D
445
F34

Fallers, Lloyd A.

The social
anthropology of the
nation-state

| DATE | | | |
|------|---|---|---|
| APR 6 '78 | | | |
| MAY 1 1 '78 | | | |
| | | | |
| | | | |
| | | | |
| | | | |
| | | | |
| | | | |
| | | | |
| | | | |
| | | | |

# THE SOCIAL ANTHROPOLOGY OF THE NATION-STATE

*THE LEWIS HENRY MORGAN LECTURES / 1971*

*presented at*

*The University of Rochester*

*Rochester, New York*

# THE SOCIAL ANTHROPOLOGY OF THE NATION-STATE

LLOYD A. FALLERS
*The University of Chicago*

 *Aldine Publishing Company, Chicago*

ABOUT THE AUTHOR

Lloyd A. Fallers (1925-1974) was A.A. Michelson Distinguished Service Professor of Anthropology and Sociology at the University of Chicago. He received his Ph.B., M.A. and Ph.D. in Anthropology at the University of Chicago. He was a Fellow and Director of the East African Institute of Social Research, had taught at Princeton University and the University of California at Berkeley, had done extensive field research in East Africa and Turkey, and was a member of the Commission on Land Tenure for the government of Basutoland. Professor Fallers was Associate Editor for Anthropology of the *International Encyclopedia of the Social Sciences,* and the author of many reviews, articles and sections of books. Among his several books is *Law Without Precedent: Legal Ideas in Action in the Courts of Colonial Busoga.*

First published 1974 by
Aldine Publishing Company
529 South Wabash Avenue
Chicago, Illinois 60605

ISBN 0-202-01128-3 clothbound edition
Library of Congress Catalog Number 74-76548
Printed in the United States of America

*To Audrey Richards
and Edward Shils*

# CONTENTS

# FOREWORD

The Lewis Henry Morgan Lectures, presented at The University of Rochester annually since 1963, serve to commemorate the man and his work.[1] They also provide the Lecturer with an opportunity to explore, summarize and examine developments since Morgan's time, or to present new views.

In the set of Lectures offered here, Professor Fallers offers a stimulating discussion of nation–states considered in the framework of social anthropology, making skillful use of his own work in East Africa and in Turkey.

Anthropologists familiar with the work of Morgan will note many connections with it — and also many departures. Those who have followed Professor Fallers' career will recognize in this book elements of what has gone before, skillfully combined with much that is new and provocative. What is presented here will certainly stimulate debate, and will provide important points of departure for anthropologists concerned

1. Brief remarks on the connection of Lewis Henry Morgan with The University of Rochester, and on the initiation of the Morgan Lectures in 1963, are to be found in the Foreword to Professor Meyer Fortes' *Kinship and the Social Order* (Aldine, 1969).

with a very wide range of problems.

All who heard Professor Fallers present his Lectures, or who discussed his work with him in seminars and in less formal circumstances, will recall with pleasure his relaxed tolerance in face of divergent views, and his eagerness to join others in exploring still further. With his lectures in print, it will make it possible for a larger audience to appreciate this most recent example of his wide-ranging scholarship.

The 1971 Lewis Henry Morgan Lectures were delivered on April 6th to 15th. This volume is a revision of the original Lectures, and to them, Professor Fallers has added a concluding chapter.

ALFRED HARRIS
*Department of Anthropology*
*University of Rochester*

# PREFACE

It is indeed an honor to be invited to deliver the Lewis Henry Morgan lectures, honoring one of the founders of the anthropological discipline, and especially to be invited to speak in succession to Fred Eggan, Meyer Fortes, Floyd Lounsbury and all the others who have set such an intimidatingly high standard for this occasion.

In speaking on the subject I have chosen, "The Social Anthropology of the Nation–State," on Morgan's home ground and in a series honoring him, I am sensible of being in somewhat contentious dialogue with a man of another time and of a different turn of mind: his age was a more optimistic one than our own and Morgan himself more optimistic than I, at any rate, felt it easy to be with respect to contemporary civilization. Morgan saw the modern democratic nation–state as the culmination of human political experience — a revival of, and an improvement upon, the political institutions of classical antiquity and its antecedents (see Morgan 1871:351-52). If the nation–state seems to many of us today a more problematical achievement, it is because the intervening century has left us sadder, if not wiser, about the results of modern man's efforts to govern himself in a civilized manner. At the same time, I take heart from Morgan's interest in these matters. If he viewed democracy from an excessively materialistic and evolutionary perspective — a perspective with which I shall have occasion in these lectures to quarrel — I nevertheless take courage from his belief that a social anthropologist might have something useful to say about the subject — about the nature of ". . . that form of self-government which represents and expresses the average intelligence and virtue of a free and educated people" (Morgan 1871:344).

I should like to express my gratitude to members of the Department of Anthropology at the University of Rochester, especially to Alfred and Grace Harris, Gerald and Andria Williams, Rene and Clara Millon, Walter and Cindy Sangree and Allan and Sue Hoben for their gracious hospitality during my two weeks in Rochester. They were also good enough to give me useful criticisms of the lectures which have, I believe, improved them. I should also like to thank others who have provided helpful criticism: Edward Shils, Margaret Fallers, Reinhard Bendix, Clifford Geertz, Lawrence Rosen, Michael Meeker, Dale Eichelman, James Siegel, Fahir İz, Leonard Binder and Elizabeth Calkins. Much of the stimulus for the ideas presented here was provided by colleagues in the weekly seminar of the Committee for the Comparative Study of New Nations at the University of Chicago, especially Clifford Geertz, Aristide Zolberg, Morris Janowitz, Philip Foster, Nur Yalman and Manning Nash. I am particularly indebted to my teacher and colleague, Edward Shils. For twenty-five years he has been for me a source of enlightenment and inspiration in his devotion to the study of the interrelations among civility, liberty and justice. The influence of his work pervades these lectures; indeed, as I submit them for publication, I have the uncomfortable suspicion that there is little here that he did not teach me about their subject.

I must also record my lasting debt to Audrey Richards for what she taught me in London and East Africa. Under her leadership the East African Institute for Social Research provided a stimulating environment for research and the discussion of research on East African societies.

Finally, I am most grateful to the agencies and foundations whose financial support enabled me to carry out research in East Africa and Turkey: the Fulbright Program, the Colonial Development and Welfare Fund, the Carnegie Corporation, the Rockefeller Foundation and the National Science Foundation.

# THE SOCIAL
# ANTHROPOLOGY
# OF THE
# NATION-STATE

# one

# MICROCOSMS AND MACROCOSMS

> The age of nationalism represents the first period
> of *universal* history. What preceded it, was the long
> era of *separate* civilizations and continents among
> which little, if any, intercourse or contact existed.
>
> The seventeenth century is the great divide be-
> tween the age in which all political and social con-
> cepts bear the decisive impress of the religious and
> universalist tradition, and an era in which the po-
> litical idea of nationalism, secular and parochial,
> becomes dominant and creates its own symbols for
> the integration of human thoughts and emotions.
>
> HANS KOHN, 1944
> *The Idea of Nationalism*

The contemporary nation–state, erected upon the sentiment
of nationalism, is an ambiguous political phenomenon. It often
unites what was formerly diverse and scattered, but often, too,
it creates particularism where formerly there was universality.
It is popular in that it rests upon mutual identification between
rulers and ruled based upon common primordial qualities —
qualities which are felt to be ancient, inherent, given, however
new they may in fact be: language, territory, culture, race.[1] But
it has produced far more rigorous authoritarianisms, and fre-

---

1. This term, as well as much of the tenor of the following discussion,
comes from Shils (1957) and from Geertz (1963). The term "primordial" has
been criticized on the ground that the social bonds and cultural unities in
question are often not at all ancient, but on the contrary are demonstrably
quite recent. For example, several million persons in eastern Nigeria "discovered," with the help of ideologists, ethnographers and colonial ad-

*(Continued on page 2)*

1

quently less tolerance of diversity, than the old kingdoms and empires ever did. While nation–states divide the world into more numerous absolute sovereignties than did preceding political forms, their broad similarities are nearly world–wide in ideal constitutional conception, and to a great extent in actual institutional structure. Extravagantly celebrated as the people's liberator, excoriated as spendthrift of the people's blood from the Wilderness to Verdun to Stalingrad and beyond, the nation–state within an international system of nation–states remains in our time a fundamental feature of the human condition, in spite of widespread aspiration to a more firmly–based international order.

Nevertheless, today the nation–state is in trouble virtually everywhere. The new excolonial states which have emerged from the disintegration of the late medieval and modern empires, as well as the residual metropolitan centers of those empires, generally began life assuming that these new units would be generally homogeneous socially and culturally and therefore united politically. But despite realignment of boundaries and vast movements of populations, both spontaneous and planned, both peaceful and bloody; and despite strenuous efforts at "national education" and propoganda, it has proved impossible either to wipe out the diversities that are the residue of history or to prevent new ones from developing through

---

ministrators that they were all Ibo only during the British colonial period. This new unity, however, once discovered, became very strong, forming the basis for the Biafran secession movement a few years after independence. "Material interests" of course became involved, as they commonly do in such situations, but this does not alter the fact that the community on behalf of which these interests were asserted *had come to think of itself* as a primordial one. The point may be further illustrated by the term "customary law," often defined by legal scholars as unwritten law that has existed since "time immemorial." Social anthropological studies of such law have found it to be in constant flux; those who use it, however, often feel it to be fixed and ancient.

migration or internal differentiation.

For example, neither the Greeks remaining in Turkey nor the Turks still in Greece have become true citizens (in more than a legal sense) of the countries within whose boundaries they reside. The totalitarian successor–states of the Austro–Hungarian and Russian empires sit precariously upon severe "nationality" problems. Great Britain still wrestles with the internal, as well as the external, consequences of her very first overseas colonial venture as well as with those of later ones, despite post imperial efforts to return to a more narrowly British or English sense of nationality. On the other hand her liberated territories in Asia and Africa, like those of France, struggle to create common loyalties within boundaries that once made imperial, but do not now make national sense. Imperial boundaries, the result of the economic and strategic rivalries of metropolitan powers, frequently both threw together very diverse groups and divided areas of cultural homogeneity. In the states of the New World and Australasia, indigenes, imported slaves and bondsmen, and voluntary immigrants of many kinds have all retained distinct identities, loyalties and prejudices. Even little Belgium's unity sometimes seems as precarious as that of her great excolony in Africa. And so it goes; the list is far too long to complete.

The logic of populistic nationalism, when it rises to self–consciousness, insists upon unity based upon similarity, but this very insistence encourages scrutiny to discover and eradicate diversity and thus exacerbates disunity. So it is that nation–states are more civil when they are less self–consciously national.

The tension between differentiation and common citizenship is not, or course, a product of primordial ties alone. Religion, which in some situations fuses in peoples' minds with language, ethnicity or race and consequently assumes a primordial or given character, is equally capable of dissolving older identities and solidarities and of creating new ones.[2] Such major bases of social and cultural differentiation as class, occupation, education and even age and sex (age and sex are of course primordial in a somewhat different sense) may become self-conscious and emerge as important sources of insistent identity and solidarity, cross-cutting culture, language and race. Thus the national state is not "one and indivisible," despite the frequent claims of its spokesmen that it is so.

In its times of civic quietude, all these fault lines, as well as self-conscious identification with the nation-state itself, recede into the background of its people's daily lives, which then proceed, for the most part, in terms of the personal ties of neighborhood and work place, sociability and routine worship. But such times alternate with periods of heightened self-consciousness of more distant, diverse and generalized loyalties which in quiet times lie dormant. Directed externally, the sentiment of national loyalty may occasionally supersede all others, uniting the citizens in something approximating the shoulder-to-shoulder brotherhood to which they are so commonly summoned by the music, ritual and icons of nation-states. More commonly, since nation-states are internally differentiated in so many dimensions, heightened self-consciousness causes diverse solidarities to stimulate each other by opposition, to challenge each other and may even threaten the integrity of the nation-state itself if these solidarities, felt to be crucial, are insufficiently represented in the politics and culture of the state. Then the most routine acts of everyday life may become heavy with larger meaning. A song, a sporting event, an item of clothing or a church bell may become an incitement to conflict, the family car a sign board

2. These possibilities, among others, are nicely adumbrated with respect to Christianity in H. Richard Niebuhr's *Christ and Culture* (1951).

for slogans. Citizens come to regard each other warily and to make exorbitant demands upon each other's civility.[3] Everyday interaction with neighbor and workmate becomes uneasy and harsh — a continuing negotiation of fresh social contracts. The common use of public space is threatened; insult, or even violence, lurks behind every misstep or misunderstanding.

Nikos Kazantzakis, in his novels about Greek life in the late Ottoman empire, has brilliantly portrayed the alternation between routine and extraordinary times as two nations, over the course of more than a century, emerged from the crumbling imperial structure in a series of bloody spasms. Even late in the nineteenth century, when this process was far advanced, life went on, most of the time, with little consciousness of ethnic difference. In *Freedom and Death* (1966), set in Kazantzakis' native Crete which was still Ottoman, the Greek Metropolitan and the Turkish Pasha could still exchange routine courtesies and Nuri Bey and Captain Michaelis could still become blood brothers. But the crescendo of national consciousness was rising and an incident in a coffee house or an illicit interethnic flirtation could shatter personal bonds and set off a blood bath.

The process may, of course, move in the opposite direction — toward greater unity *and* greater civility through events which reduce the divisiveness of diversity. Without pretending to evaluate the tragically brief presidency of the late John F. Kennedy, one may say that it substantially increased religious tolerance, and hence civility, in the United States. His victory at the polls (narrow though it was), his careful handling of the religious issue while in office and his death in the prime of life and the days of national mourning which followed may well have put to rest the old Protestant fantasies about the dangers of "popery" in the White House. The image and the rasping

3. By "civility" I mean a tolerant and generous recognition of common attachment to, and responsibility for, the social order, despite diversity.

Irish voice of a grandfatherly Boston cardinal, projected into millions of Protestant homes by television, converted the Roman Catholic requiem mass from a dangerous cabalistic rite into an accepted expression of religion in America. To Roman Catholics all this gave a greater ease and self-confidence. The heroic life and martyr's death of Martin Luther King perhaps helped to ameliorate the much more deep-seated and intractable prejudice of racism.

We in this country are today, nevertheless, in a state of extraordinary consciousness of competing identities and solidarities. There are few nation-states that do not share this condition to some degree. Its causes — some obvious, others obscure — are complex and beyond the scope of this discussion. I do not regard it as inevitable; I do not, for reasons I shall spell out later, believe in historical inevitability. I do suggest, though, that the nation-state that attempts to combine relatively high levels of popular participation in public affairs with great diversities in primordial sentiment, occupation, wealth, religion and style of life makes heavier demands upon the civility of its citizens and the creativity of its politicians than we have commonly acknowledged. It is in the nature of social ties and cultural commitments that they be stubbornly defended by those who hold them. Civility therefore requires some surrender of the very essence of the sociocultural self; and leadership in the interest of civility requires self-restraint, a willingness to forego the easy appeal to less generous sentiments, and an effort to create a political culture within which the inevitable conflicts of interest and sentiment may be played out without excessive surrender of ties and commitments by any substantial portion of the citizens. Just because it runs against the grain of sociocultural man, such a political culture is unstable and vulnerable; it requires constant and careful tending.

But what has anthropology to do with all of this? The "study of man," for all the immodesty of its name, has concerned itself almost exclusively with man in small groups: bands, tribal segments, village communities, and, recently, urban neighborhoods, schools and work places. In the division of labor of the social sciences (insofar as the social sciences possess a division of labor), social anthropology has been the science of the sociocultural microcosm and has developed a method and style of inquiry appropriate to this task. Whatever new gadgets and techniques may have been added to it, anthropological "fieldwork," even when carried out in an affluent suburb or in a steel mill, still fundamentally consists of the participant–observational study of small groups of men and women in social interaction. It seeks to grasp both (a) the complexes of belief and value which render meaningful to those who engage in them the various patterns of social action in a microcosm and (b) the functions, or consequences, of these patterns of action for each other in the flow of social life. For this purpose it cultivates the arts of communication — the mastery of languages and other symbol systems which are the vehicles of meaning.

For example, at the newsstand on a street corner in my neighborhood there is always to be found a small group of men in addition to the proprietor. Today, while buying my paper, I see Alfred hand Sam a substantial sum of money. What does this transaction mean to Alfred and to Sam? Is Alfred: (a) repaying a loan? (b) engaging in philanthropy? (c) placing a bet with a bookie? I can only know when I understand the language and gesture of social action within this particular microcosm. Again, what are the social consequences of this and other transactions of the same sort? Are they: (a) people here are the prey of loan sharks? (b) people here are generous to the poor? (c) people here waste their money betting on the horses and so sometimes cannot feed and clothe their children? I can know only when I follow up the consequences of this and other similar transactions in the lives of those who engage in them. Questions of the first sort tell me what Alfred and Sam intend by their action. Of course the two of them may not see the transaction in the same light. Assuming that Sam is a bookie, Alfred may regard the placing of a bet as an act of philanthropy, since he himself is not a habitual gambler but knows Sam to be down on his luck; Sam, on the other hand, may regard it as strictly a business transaction. Answering the second sort of question — concerning function or consequence — involves finding out what in fact happens, whatever the actors' intentions, both in the particular case of Alfred and Sam and also more generally (since Alfred and Sam may be merely a couple of social deviants whose actions have individual rather than social significance). In order to learn about all these matters, the fieldworker cultivates especially the receptive side of communication — the ability to spend most of one's time listening instead of speaking, watching instead of acting; he learns to remember and to record in great detail what he sees and hears. These are difficult disciplines requiring rigorous training for academic intellectuals, who usually would rather talk than listen and who find boring or repulsive what they see as the "trivia" of ordinary life, particularly in their own societies.

As the science of the sociocultural microcosm, anthropology is thus the science of "intersubjectivity," as phenomenologists like to call it, in its natural habitat, at the grass roots. The human capacity for intersubjectivity — for what George Herbert Mead (1934) called "taking the role of the other" — is what provides the fieldworker with his data: meaningful social action. It is Alfred and Sam's ability to view the situation from

implicit cultural orientation or "background" (as we say, quite appropriately for the point I wish to make), and a routine pattern of social relations provide a kind of platform, more or less stable, from which we may from time to time more self-consciously *use* our beliefs and values and manipulate our social relations in shaping our biographies and in dealing with the out-of-the-ordinary. The concern with the socially and culturally ordinary in this sense leads the fieldworker to take note of matters, (e.g., turns of phrase, bodily movements, styles of dress and home furnishings, expressions of deference and hauteur, modes of sociability, attentiveness, relaxation, recreation, etc.) that to other social scientists may seem trivial but that the fieldworker knows may turn out to be crucial to an understanding of the anthropology of everyday life and hence of not-so-everyday life.

They may prove significant because, finally, the field-worker's perspective is "holistic." This much-misunderstood phrase does not mean that he regards the microcosms he studies either as self-sufficient isolates or as scaled-down models of the larger society of which they are parts. Either assumption would of course be nonsensical, especially in an anthropology of the contemporary nation-state. He may not even regard them as "typical" of other such microcosms, for his particular purposes may make it useful to choose microcosms in which some particular features are heightened, thus providing a deeper understanding of those features' more general significance in the society. For example, there may be reason to regard a microcosm as avant-garde or conservative with respect to a particular feature. In the first case the fieldworker may gain some insight into the direction in which other such microcosms may be moving; in the second he may learn something about where they have been. Again, highly specialized microcosms may tell him something about much more common ones. In a training school for priests, where concern with religious matters is much more self-conscious, one may learn things that help one to understand the interaction between priest and people in an ordinary congregation. There are many possible complexities here, of course, but the usefulness of the holistic perspective does not depend upon them.

This perspective consists, rather, in the understanding of the sociocultural worlds[7] of typical actors involved in particular sorts of microcosms. These microcosms will seldom be completely coextensive, as among different actors, particularly in a complex society, though typical clusterings may be expected. For example, my neighbor and I share two microcosms, since we happen to be colleagues, but we also inhabit microcosms peculiar to each of us. But the assumption underlying the holistic study of microcosms is that such units, or typical clusterings, for all their lack of closure, have an organized, systemic quality — an interconnectedness among their elements — which has significance for the larger society through its significance in the lives of its members. A neighborhood, a work place, a school, a voluntary association — each has a life of its own. Each influences, and is influenced by, the persons who pass through it in the round of life and in the course of life.

It should now be clear, in a general way, how social anthropological inquiry relates to the study of the nation-state. The class, religious and other cleavages which differentiate its citizens appear in everyday life in the structure of the complexes of microcosms — in the ways in which microcosms typically overlap, or fail to overlap, both among themselves and with primordial solidarities. Class, religion and primordial

7. This discussion owes a good deal to the writings of Schutz (1962, 1967) and to those of Berger and Luckman (1966). I make no effort at this point, however, to collate my terminology with theirs.

identities are not themselves microcosms, but they enter into the worlds of meaning which inform social interaction within microcosms, ordinarily in an implicit, muted way, but potentially and sporadically in a much more self–conscious way. The microcosms of work place, neighborhood and voluntary association may, of course, be in varying degrees either homogeneous or heterogeneous with respect to these identities and solidarities; this has a bearing upon the latters' potentiality for self–consciousness, since self–consciousness in one person tends to stimulate self–consciousness in others. The several microcosms inhabited by a person together make up his round of everyday life and provide the background against which he acts, or is acted upon, as a citizen of the nation–state. Examples will be given in later chapters.

Thus far I have spoken of the fieldworker's role in the study of the nation–state in a quite descriptive way, seeking to convey something of his manner of work and the kind of information it yields. Before considering its complementarities with other modes of research on the subject it is appropriate here to make a short detour into the larger intellectual context in which our studies of national societies and their polities proceed.

As increasing numbers of social anthropologists have undertaken research into the more complex contemporary societies — especially in connection with the post–Second World War concern with the emergence of national states in former colonial territories, though the movement began somewhat earlier — they have been drawn into contact with what may be called the comparative macrosociological tradition, a tradition of thought which grew out of the efforts of Western intellectuals to interpret (and often to further) the "great transformation" of their own societies from medieval kingdoms and principalities into modern nation–states. Choosing a rather arbitrary starting point and touching only a few of the most important bases along the way, we may say that the tradition developed from the secularization of political thought and the development of the idea of sovereignty, through the Enlightenment celebration of reason as against custom, through the economists' theory of the politically autonomous business firm and into the nineteenth century efflorescence of typological and evolutionary conceptualizations of history.[8] Throughout these discussions past (which is to say medieval) sociocultural forms are contrasted with those thought to be emerging. Most writers in this tradition have preferred the new, though there is, of course, particularly in the nineteenth century, a counter theme of conservative, in the sense of anti–modernist, thought which generally agrees with the evolutionists about the trend of history while maintaining a skeptical, if not hostile attitude toward its results.[9] All this eventuates in the turn–of–the–century work of Durkheim, Pareto and Weber (and of course a penumbra of lesser figures[10]), each in his way concerned with the

8. Machiavelli and, in more radical terms, Hobbes, seem to be most responsible for the notion that the state is a product of human artifice, not of divine ordination. God creates man; man creates the state (and/or society). That being the case, the state and the social order generally are proper objects for secular inquiry. Bodin's development of the idea of sovereignty — the notion of a political community which is quite autonomous of others and which possesses a center in which ultimate authority resides — is probably the proximate source of the idea of society as a bounded system. Organic conceptions of state and society were common in the Middle Ages, but these conceptions were suffused with notions of divine ordination, while Bodin was, like Hobbes and Machiavelli, a secularizer of sociopolitical thought. See Gierke (1958) and Bertrand de Jouvenel, *Sovereignty* (1957).

The philosophers of the Enlightenment are too numerous and too well–known to list. So are the economists, though of course Adam Smith and Ricardo stand as the dominant figures. Marx, Spencer, Comte and Maine are perhaps the most influential figures in mid–nineteenth–century evolutionary and typological thought.

9. I have in mind here such diverse celebrants of received culture and institutions as Burke, Tocqueville and Mathew Arnold.

10. Ferdinand Tönnies, Marcel Mauss, C.H. Cooley and W.I. Thomas were concerned, to one degree or another, with similar problems.

following problem: the "great transformation" has loosened the bonds of custom and tradition, has released and even institutionalized individualism and rationality, yet how is it that in some sense custom and tradition remain? Talcott Parsons, in his *The Structure of Social Action* (1937), has shown how each of these men contributed to what Parsons calls the "voluntaristic theory of action" — a conceptual scheme in which purposive rationality is seen as operating within customary, consensual normative, or moral, frameworks. That is to say, the "great transformation" involves not the dissolution by reason of moral order as such, but rather the institution of new "rationalistic" moral orders — in the market economy, in the bureaucratic state, in the institutions of scientific and technological research. Each of these orders presupposes a system of values in which systematic productivity, administrative efficiency or the pursuit of knowledge and control of nature become ends in themselves.

Now it happened that at the very period when this critical synthetic work was in progress in comparative macrosociology, anthropologists were disengaging themselves from that tradition and proceeding in a quite different direction — away from grand synthesis and toward ethnographic empiricism. Whereas a few decades earlier the evolutionary perspective had linked the investigators of the simpler societies (E.B. Tylor, for example, and Lewis Henry Morgan) with the students of the Western "great transformation" (the evolutionary anthropologists showed the latter that theirs was only the latest in a series of such transformations), now Franz Boas and Bronislaw Malinowski, perhaps the two most influential figures in early twentieth century anthropology in the United States and Britain respectively, were in revolt against grand historical theory in both its evolutionary and its diffusionist forms. They rejected the effort to relate the societies conventionally studied by anthropologists to the "civilized" world through general theories of history, usually on the ground that such theories were excessively speculative, that their hypotheses were inherently untestable on the basis of available evidence, though Boas and Malinowski had positive reasons as well for abandoning such preoccupations. If they disagreed about much else, they were at one in their empiricism and relativism — in their insistence that each society be studied intensively, directly and "on its own terms." Both were deeply interested in developing field methods for ferreting out the worlds of meaning in which preliterate peoples lived and each may be said to have produced in his own country the first generation of professional, academic anthropological fieldworkers.[11]

Thus, while comparative macrosociologists were achieving a new synthesis for the conceptualization of contemporary national societies, anthropologists were busy inventing, codifying and institutionalizing the fieldworker's craft. "Inventing" is of course too strong a word. There had already been isolated individuals — travelers, colonial administrators, missionaries and gentlemen scholars — who had done excellent fieldwork. Certainly among the best of these autodidacts was Lewis Henry Morgan, who, a half-century earlier, in addition to his evolutionary speculations, was a meticulous investigator of the institutions of the Iroquois, in my view a much more valuable contribution. But it was the generation of Malinowski and Boas who made the first-hand study of small-scale

11. It should be noted that there is a quite parallel tradition in the nineteenth centruy of "fieldwork" among the poor of the western world which also begins with amateur "exploration" and gradually becomes more systematized into the statistical survey on the one hand and what has come to be called urban social anthropology on the other. Thus Henry Mayhew, whose *London Labor and the London Poor* appeared in 1861-62, describes his work as an effort to present the condition of the poor "from the lips of the people themselves," "in their own unvarnished language" and likens himself to James Bruce, the explorer of Ethiopia.

societies a systematic discipline. Their students and their students' students refined it and conceptualized it as the "holistic" study of what I have termed sociocultural micro-systems.

Thus anthropologists who, beginning in the 1930s and 1940s and in larger numbers ever since, came to the study of large-scale national societies, did so with a splendid craft tradition but with a conceptual apparatus which was quite out of touch with recent developments in macrosociology. There were exceptions: One was Robert Redfield, one of my own teachers, who had received his anthropological training in a joint sociology-anthropology department. And some very fruitful work was accomplished by some who never fully transcended the contemporary anthropological perspective. Among these was William Lloyd Warner, another of my teachers, who gave to the study of social stratification in the United States a cultural dimension which it had previously lacked. But the effort to articulate the two perspectives satisfactorily has required substantial time and effort and is still in progress. In the process, naturally enough, many crudities have been committed, the commonest being the assumption that a contemporary nation-state may be viewed, simply, as a cluster of sociocultural microcosms — usually a residential community — writ large, a limitation from which Warner's early work sometimes suffered. Another common false assumption is the one that anthropological concepts and methods are particularly suited to "traditional" (in the sense of custom-bound) societies, while those of political scientists and sociologists are more appropriate to "modern" societies. This is a relic of nineteenth century typological and evolutionary thought which has inhibited the necessary synthesis.

But the anthropological perspective cannot be brought into a fruitful working relationship with the macrosociological either by peaceful coexistence or by dividing up and sharing out the world's societies. My own view is that true synthesis requires something more and that Max Weber's version of the macrosociological perspective provides the most promising initial point of articulation, as the vocabulary of my earlier discussion of life in the microcosm will no doubt have suggested. In Weber's formulation, outlined in the first part of his *Economy and Society* (1968) and applied in his wide-ranging comparative studies, the terms "tradition" and "rationality" are used at two levels of analysis. At the macroscopic level he speaks, for example, of the "traditional authority" of kings, as contrasted with the "rational-legal authority" of bureaucratic officials. At the level of individual "orientations to action," he contrasts "traditional" with "rational action." In the first case he is talking about the mode of legitimation of authority — its ideological justification. Thus traditional authority is justified. by its time-hallowedness, rational-legal authority by its legalistic logicality. On the level of individual social action, he is concerned with the degree of self-consciousness with which action is undertaken. Traditionally-oriented action is habitual, customary and unreflective, while rationally-oriented action is relatively explicit, self-conscious in its purposiveness. The two levels must not be confused, for the actions of the most traditionally-legitimated king and his servants may be quite "rational," in the sense of explicit, in asserting the "traditional" legitimacy of their authority and in pursuing their objectives within that framework by the most efficient available means, while much of the action that goes on within the most legalistically rational civil service or business enterprise may be quite habitual and customary.

And indeed, Weber would say, it must be so since human beings everywhere and at all times are capable of only partial and sporadic self-conscious attention to their purposes. Alfred Schutz has built upon these ideas of Weber's, enriching our conceptual equipment for analyzing the way in which implicit culture and habitual social expectations provide, as I noted earlier, a background against which, and in terms of which, sporadic attention may be given to events or "projects" outside the stream of everyday life in the microcosm and to events which intrude into it (Schutz 1962, 1967). He thus develops conceptual links between Weber's discussion of action orientations and the scheme of institutional ideal types which make up the latter's macrosociology.

To return, now, to the relationship between the data of social anthropological fieldwork and those acquired through other methods and informed by other perspectives, I suggest that, in concerning itself with the un-self-conscious culture and social organization of everyday life in which from the point of view, say, of a political scientist nothing is happening most of the time, the microcosmic view nevertheless contributes something to an understanding of a nation's political life that cannot be gotten from other standpoints and methods of data-gathering. This is perhaps best indicated by contrast with two other leading approaches: the study of large-scale organizations and the analysis of standardized national aggregate data, generated either by the social scientist (as in attitude or opinion survey research) or by the state itself (as in the case of demographic and electoral statistics). Both are peculiarly relevant — indeed crucial — to the study of the nation-state and, in the case of state statistics, of course, products of it. Man has lived in sociocultural microcosms since the Pleistocene. He has lived in large-scale organizations and in "mass societies" for only the past two hundred years or so.

In earlier times there were, of course, large-scale organizations in the sense of social units deliberately created for particular purposes and employing the services of large numbers of persons. In the medieval West the essential ones

were church and state. In the ancient and medieval empires —
Roman, Ottoman and Chinese among others — state
organization was still more self-consciously purposive and
far-flung. On a smaller scale, the kingdom-states of some
regions of Africa, Southeast Asia and Middle and South
America were tightly organized and highly active in the pursuit
of expansion and plunder. But contemporary government in
the nation-state is far more active than any of these and its
capacity regularly to impinge upon the microcosms of everyday life is far greater. And of course what is peculiarly unique
to our own times is the great multiplicity of nongovernmental
organizations which harness tens, even hundreds, of thousands
of persons in pursuit of special purposes. Such giant social
constructions as International Telephone and Telegraph, the
Brotherhood of Teamsters, the Ford Foundation, the
American Baseball League, the University of California and of
course their counterparts in other countries, direct and
coordinate the activities of large numbers of persons for
diverse purposes and through varying organizational formats,
all of which, however, have in common the utilization in some
degree of bureaucratic administration.

Students of this crucial feature of the life of the contemporary nation-state clearly cannot rely solely, or even largely,
on fieldwork techniques. One cannot study an elephant armed
only with a microscope. Much of the data must come from
documentary sources and from highly specialized
interviewing. But the microscopic view is relevant — I would
say essential — in the case of the large-scale organization, as in
that of the elephant. For if the organization lives (let us now
drop the elephant lest I be trampled by my own metaphor) in
the complex flow of formal, highly explicit and specific communication, its members live in a many-faceted sociocultural

world in which the organization is only one element — though perhaps a crucial one — among others. And even within the organization, its formal, self-consciously purposive operations are mediated through the sociocultural microcosms, interlaced with internal and external personal ties, that form the setting for day-to-day work life. Modern methods of communication and organization give the general manager a wider and more detailed view of the whole, and hence a broader span of control, than that possessed by the medieval king, bishop or governor. However, even an administrative virtuoso like Robert McNamara, whether at the Ford Motor Company, the Department of Defense or the World Bank, is far from occupying the position of god–like omniscience and omnipotence envisaged by Jeremy Bentham for the chief of his panopticon,[12] for even his office, as work place, is a microcosm of personal ties, as is every other work place up and down the line.

National aggregate statistics are products of the age of the nation–state in a more direct sense. They, by definition, represent aspects of the national whole. A great many of them — most notably the census — are directly generated by contemporary governments in pursuit of their organizational purposes — purposes which in many cases would be ludicrously over-ambitious without the information they provide. Survey research which purports to say something about the national whole depends upon the census and other

12. "— a circular prison where one inspector — is in a position to supervise all the cells which are arranged concentrically round a central pavillion; a system of blinds makes invisible the inspector who sees everything. — 'to be incessantly under the eyes of the inspector is to lose in effect the power to do evil and almost the thought of wanting to do it.'—. He recommended that the principle be extended to factories, mad–houses, hospitals and even to schools—" Halévy (1955:82-85).

data produced by governmental operations in the construction
of its samples. The quantity of statistical data thus generated
by and about nation–states — particularly the more
"developed" ones — is huge and ever–growing.

Censuses were taken, of course, before there were
nation–states. The eleventh century social and economic
survey which produced the Domesday Book, in which William
the Conqueror's agents recorded in marvelous (for that time)
detail the resources, human and nonhuman, which he had won
from Harold on the field of Hastings, is the example most
familiar to us, but many of the old kingdoms and empires
counted people and things, usually for fiscal and military
purposes. Nevertheless, the data generated by contemporary
censuses, elections, taxation and a host of special inves-
tigations and registration requirements are of an entirely
different order of magnitude and accuracy. Kant caught an
early glimpse of their possibilities when he wrote, in his "Idea
for a Universal History with Cosmopolitan Intent" (1786):

> Thus marriages, the consequent births and the deaths, since the
> free will seems to have such a great influence upon them, do not
> seem to be subject to any law according to which one could
> calculate their number beforehand. Yet the annual (statistical)
> tables about them in the major countries show that they occur ac-
> cording to stable natural laws. (pp. 116-31)

Like many after him he was led by this observation to wistful
talk about a new Newton or Kepler for the social sciences who
would discover the "perfect civic constitution."

National aggregate statistics do indeed represent the
nation–state's attempt to take stock of itself and better itself,
though Kant would have been disappointed to know how
much more difficult improvement has proved to be than
assessment. But governmentally–generated statistical data
view the nation–state in a particular way. By themselves they

produce only quantity and classification, and the same is generally true of survey data. They produce, as Kant observed, tables. By themselves they tell us only the characteristics of the populations by individual or by household. They tell us, for example, what proportion of white industrial workers between the ages of twenty-one and thirty voted for Henry Wallace in 1948 or George Wallace in 1968. This is no mean accomplishment as anyone knows who has tried to make sense of election results in countries for which such data are lacking. But they cannot tell us why the persons in question voted as they did — "why" in the sense of what voting in that way *meant* to them, out of what microcosmic worlds of meaning they acted. If one does not know what those voters saw in the 1948 or the 1968 Wallace, one has only the kind of understanding of them that the experimental psychologist has about his rats. Yet the more that large-scale survey studies attempt to probe for "reasons," the more doubtful their results often become. The more elaborately qualitative a standardized questionnaire, the less likely that it will mean to the respondent what it meant to its author, even though they may share the same mother tongue, for the structure of the interconnected set of questions may assume a logic which is not present in the sociocultural microcosm of the respondent. I was made painfully aware of this in my own work in an East African society when I attempted to administer a questionnaire about "social class." Although I had already done two years' fieldwork in the society and ought to have known better, I simply translated questions of the sort used by sociologists in the United States into the African language. The questionnaire was almost meaningless to the people I interviewed because, as it turned out, the pyramid and layer cake imagery in terms of which Americans, both social scientists and others, think about social stratification (such notions as "the upper crust," "the bottom of

the heap," and "the social ladder" illustrate what I mean) simply did not exist in the culture. It was, however, rich in conceptions of dyadic relations of superiority and subordination of
the "master and servant" type, for there were great differences
of wealth, power and prestige.

Census and survey research must assume what their very ac-
complishments in constructing samples belie. That is, they
must, in asking standard questions, assume a common
national world of meaning in a population which they
themselves reveal to be so intricately differentiated in ways that
*must* imply — and fieldwork confirms it — a great diversity of
microcosmic worlds and subcultures. Furthermore, by questioning samples of individual persons, they take out of the
context of microcosmic social networks what some of them
have shown to depend upon that context. (I have in mind here
the studies of Lazarsfeld, Berelson and Gaudet [1948] on voting behavior.) In short, they assume in their operations a
culturally homogeneous society of social atoms — a "mass
society" — where we know, and survey researchers know,
something quite different exists, something much more
pluralistic and differentiated.

Fieldwork studies of sociocultural microcosms may be of
some assistance here in surmounting some of the difficulties of
census and attitude survey research. Actually, the two modes
of investigation are complementary. National aggregate data
help the fieldworker to locate his microcosm in the national
whole and may suggest the existence of important microcosms
of which he is unaware. Fieldwork studies may reveal to the
census–taker or survey–researcher better ways of asking questions so that they will indeed mean what he wants them to
mean. But this complementarity is too rarely made use of. The
"pretesting" of questions which is supposed to achieve this
result is very often too superficial to reveal the relevant

sociocultural diversity which exists both among the respondents, and between the respondents and the researcher.
For his part, the fieldworker too often selects his microcosms
in ways which give his observations much less relevance for
macroscopic analysis than they might have had if he had
familiarized himself with the theories and data of social scientists of other perspectives.

For sometimes survey research works, spectacularly.
Sometimes there are checks that show it to work. The most
familiar and impressive example, of course, is pre-election
polling. Despite the incredible diversity of the population of
the United States, the pollsters feel humiliated if they miss by
more than a couple of percentage points. Of course the prediction of action from questioning is very short-run here, but the
most striking point about these studies is not that people do, a
week or two later, what they said they would do, nor that the
statisticians are able to produce a sample of a few thousands
that will accurately represent tens of millions — although to a
statistical innocent like myself that is impressive enough. What
is most telling is that an incredibly differentiated and scattered
array of citizens apparently *understand the questions in the
same way*. This shows that the pollsters are good at their job.
And of course the questions are rather straightforward ones involving simple choices among a few candidates or parties. The
translation problem — linguistic or cultural — is not
profound. Still, the fact that it works and the fact that the
voters generally accept the results of the subsequent election
suggests to me that the "mass society" view is at least partly
correct, at any rate, with respect to the more developed and
democratic nation-states, where elections are held and where
pollsters may operate.

The success of pre-election polling in predicting what voters
will do on election day does not, of course, show that the elec-

torate is socially and culturally homogeneous. It is precisely through an accurate understanding of its differentiation that pollsters are able to construct adequate samples. They know, and the election results confirm, that voters cast their ballots as sociocultural groups or categories, not as unpreconditioned free spirits. But if the nation–state is a loose assemblage of feuding tribes and jealous guilds, it is also unitary. The nation–state, through its electoral processes, sporadically enters into its citizens' diverse worlds of meaning, receives enough common understanding and loyalty, which is to say legitimacy, so as to bind the different tribes and guilds together, if only partially and provisionally.

Paradoxically, this seems to work best when extra–microcosmic ties and sentiments, including the sentiment of nationalism itself, are relatively quiescent. It is when primordial, class, religious, racial, national, and other loyalties which ordinarily are rather remote from consciousness come too vigorously to the fore, and when day–to–day civility declines, that interest in the electoral process deteriorates and elections may be boycotted or neglected or simply by–passed in favor of some form of direct action.

There is, I suggest, a lesson here for those who regard elections as a rather minor and unimportant aspect of the life of the nation–state — an aspect rather easily done without. Of course the state enters into its citizens' lives in many other ways, but these are mostly differentiated in terms of different categories and groups of citizens. Elections are both the great common civic rite of the nation–state and also an exercise in self–analysis. Nation–states that do without them sacrifice both a reinforcement to civility and an invaluable source of information.

My subject in these chapters, then, is the contemporary

nation-state in some of its vicissitudes — especially those for which a social anthropological perspective aids in understanding. I have attempted to characterize that perspective in both its craft and its conceptual aspects and have tried to show, again both in terms of data-gathering methods and intellectual history, how it relates to social science perspectives of other kinds. Since to continue the discussion on this general plane would be quite alien to my conception of what social anthropology — and, indeed, social science — can do best, I shall now become more particular. Such general ideas as we possess are most useful, I think, when they are applied to particular cases. In the following chapters, therefore, I shall take up some of the questions I have raised here in the context of two parts of the world of which I have some first-hand, fieldworker's knowledge: East Africa, where first colonial administrators and later nationalist leaders have attempted to create nation-states out of formerly discrete and diverse societies; and Turkey, where the nation-state is developing in the metropolitan remainder of a great polyglot empire.

First, however, I must indicate something of the nature of the data upon which these discussions will be based. My "data base" is rather different in the two "cases" in ways that follow both from their sociocultural differences and from my own knowledge of these differences. East Africa is made up of dozens of linguistic and ethnic groups which in precolonial times were politically autonomous. Its several nation-states are barely a decade old. Present-day Turkey, while not entirely homogeneous ethnically, is a great deal more so than East Africa. It has been a nation-state for half a century and was the seat of an imperial state for several hundreds of years before. While the populations of the two areas are roughly similar,

Turkey is a good deal more developed economically and weightier in international affairs.[13] Again, while Turkey is a single nation–state, East Africa is a region occupied by three, although there are good reasons for viewing the region as a unit. There are many historical links among the peoples of the various states; during the colonial period economic and political links developed which have survived, if somewhat tenuously, into the period of independence.

My first-hand experience of East Africa extended from 1950 to 1957, which is to say that it ended during the period of transition from colonial dependence to nation–statehood.[14] While I travelled rather widely throughout the entire area, my intensive fieldwork was carried out among only two of its ethnic groups — the Basoga and Baganda of Uganda. In precolonial times, Buganda had been a kingdom with a population of approximately one million and had dominated a fringe of smaller states, including the several smaller kingdoms of Busoga.[15] I carried out participant-observational studies in several areas in both Buganda and Busoga, and to a lesser extent in Kampala, the capital city of Buganda and of Uganda, a city whose population was drawn from ethnic groups throughout East Africa. But in speaking about East Africa, I am, fortunately, able to draw upon excellent work by others, for the area has

13. In 1970, Turkey's population was estimated to be 35,600,000, while that of the three East African states, taken together, was 32,700,000. Turkey's per capita income, however, was of the order of $347, while those of the East African states ranged from $120 to $60. Turkey is a member of N.A.T.O. and is negotiating for membership in the European common market, while the East African states belong to the British commonwealth and the Organization of African Unity. The population and income estimates are taken from the *New York Times Encyclopedic Almanac, 1971.*

14. Tanzania became independent in 1961, Uganda in 1962, Kenya in 1963.

15. In Bantu languages, nouns are formed by adding class prefixes to roots. Thus Basoga are the people, Busoga their country and Lusoga their language.

been well studied by social anthropologists and by other social scientists, often using fieldwork methods, both during the terminal years of colonial rule, when the politics of national states were emerging, and since that time. I can therefore know something about many microcosms which I myself have not experienced. I must depend upon them particularly for information about the last fifteen years.

My experience of Turkey is both briefer and more recent. During the past decade I have carried out a year's fieldwork in a provincial town and have spent three months each in two of the country's larger cities, including Ankara, the capital. Turkey is much easier to grasp as a whole than East Africa for two reasons: (1) despite the presence of ethnic minorities and regional variations, it possesses a national language which enables the traveler to communicate with most of its population through a single medium, and (2) it possesses a much more powerful sociocultural "center," to use Edward Shils' phrase (1961), than does East Africa either as a whole or in any of its constituent states. This is so, not only in an ecological sense — that is, transport, communications and state administration bind the ethnic and regional diversities of Turkey together much more closely — but also in a political–cultural sense. Its most salient diversities are ideological ones arising out of a nation–forming revolution experienced, in one way or another, by the great majority of the population.

On the other hand, Turkey is less well studied by social scientists, particularly on the microcosmic level. There have been a few good studies of villages, towns and urban neighborhoods, and I shall draw upon some of these, but for the most part I shall depend upon my own work on the microcosms of a single provincial town. Again, however, because of the greater volume of national aggregate data available for Turkey — a result of its greater wealth and more powerful political center — it is somewhat easier to locate these microcosms within the national whole than is the case with similar units in East Africa.

Finally, I should comment upon the quantity of historical and other information which it is necessary to provide about both East Africa and Turkey in order to construct the setting for the discussion of the contemporary interaction between microcosms and national societies. This may appear at times to overbalance the discussion of the states and their microcosms, but after all, my purpose here is not simply to celebrate social anthropological research and the understanding it yields but also to illustrate its contribution, in combination with other modes of investigation, to the understanding of the nation–state. In particular it is necessary to place the microcosms historically, for those who inhabit them act within history as experienced, both directly by themselves and, at further remove, by their predecessors and contemporaries.

# two

# EAST AFRICA: "ARTIFICIAL" NATION-STATES

We stayed one night (in Mombasa) and sailed on to the city of Kilwa, a large city on the seacoast, most of whose inhabitants are Zinj, jet-black in color . . . . The city of Kilwa is one of the finest and most substantially-built towns. . . . Its people engage in *jihad* because they are on a common mainland with the heathen Zinj people and contiguous to them, and they are for the most part religious and upright . . . .

IBN BATTUTA, 1329

. . . in the event that the proposed "closer union" is adopted it will necessarily and inevitably destroy the position and status of my kingdom. Since the interests of my people will necessarily have to be subordinated to the interests of the immigrant European races and those of other native tribes . . . .

KABAKA DAUDI CWA,
King of Buganda, 1929

The region conventionally known as "East Africa" to contemporary Europeans and Americans and as the "Land of the Zinj" to medieval Arabs comprises, roughly, the Zanzibar Islands and the adjacent mainland territory lying between the Tana river on the north and the Rovuma on the south, and stretching inland as far as the chain of mountains and lakes that divides the basin of the Congo from that of the Nile. It corresponds, again roughly, with the present–day nation–

31

states of Kenya, Uganda and Tanzania. But these states are barely a decade old, three quarters of a century old if one wishes to view the matter cartographically, and mark their lives from the time when something like their present names and boundaries were first entered on maps in European foreign offices.

The ambiguity of the macrocosms within which the peoples of this region have long lived their everyday, microcosmic lives is suggested by the two statements I have cited at the beginning of this chapter: the one by a famous Arab traveller and scholar at a time when Islamic civilization and Muslim power were dominant in the Mediterranean Sea and the Indian Ocean; the other by a shrewd inland African king, just six centuries later, when European imperialism was still virtually unchallenged throughout what was later to be called the "Third World." For Ibn Battuta, were the black-skinned "Zinj" the pious Muslim citizens of the commercial city-state of Kilwa, and thus within the world of Islam, or were they the heathen against whom *jihad* (holy war) was properly directed? Seemingly they were both (Batutta 1962:380). For Kabaka Daudi Cwa, were his people to remain primarily subjects of the Kingdom of Buganda or was Buganda, only recently amalgamated with a penumbra of other African peoples in a British "Uganda Protectorate," to have its identity further submerged in a still larger and more diverse East African federation of British dependencies (Kaizi 1948:225)? If the Turkish republican experiment in political community represents an effort to confer new civic meaning upon the residual heartland of a medieval empire, the East African political venture illustrates the effort to make civic sense out of the liberated provinces of a late Victorian one.

The peoples of the three present-day East African states, both together and individually, comprise a wide variety of in-

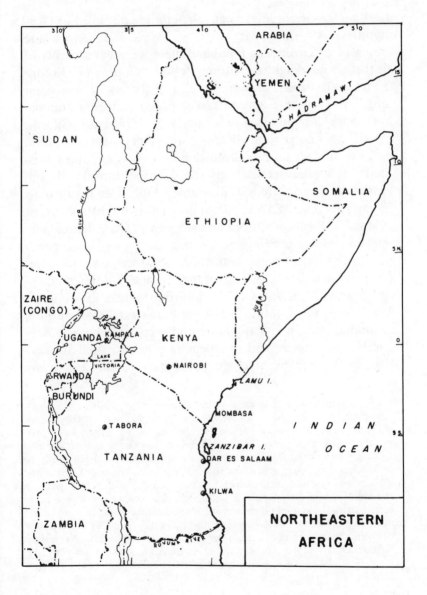

NORTHEASTERN AFRICA

digenous or precolonial linguistic, ethnic and political communities. All the great language families of Africa are
represented (Greenberg 1966) and there is a great diversity of
aesthetic and religious culture. Political communities range
from small bands of hunters and gatherers to the great
kingdoms of the interlacustrine region. Agriculture and animal
husbandry combine in a rich variety of subsistence patterns.
Upon this indigenous diversity are superimposed several
varieties of two universalistic religions — Islam and Christianity. (I shall, somewhat unjustly, ignore a third, Hinduism,
because of the socially and culturally encapsulated nature of its
Indian adherents.[1]) Also superimposed are four distinct sets of
colonial influence — three emanating from Great Britain and
one, for a time, from Germany — each leaving its own legacy of
political experience and institutions. Furthermore, this complexity or heterogeneity is not of the "mosaic" kind characteristic of parts of Southeast Asia and the Middle East (Geertz
1963), for (except in the case of the Indians) religion, culture,
economic roles, political arenas, and even kinship commonly
overlap imperfectly and interpenetrate incompletely in ways
that render highly problematical the relevance of each to any

---

1. Indians have been *in* East Africa for some time — indeed, they have
been on the coast as traders as long, perhaps, as the Arabs — but they are not
really *of* it. They have rarely intermarried with Africans and there is very little
evidence of African conversion to Hinduism. In this the Indians contrast
strikingly with the Arabs. The difference would seem to be attributable to the
sociocultural complex associated with caste which stresses endogamy and
ideas of purity and polution which preclude intimacy with non-Hindus. In
the context of modern populistic politics this has meant a resentment of Indian success in economic enterprise which has burst out in anti-Indian
movements. In Uganda General Amin and other political leaders have
deliberately exacerbated these resentments, while President Nyerere in
Tanzania has tried to play them down, but they exist at the grass-roots level
throughout the region. For an account of Indian communities in East Africa,
see Morris (1968).

given situation. In addition, the monotheistic religions are relative newcomers to the area — except, of course, for the coastal zone, where Islam is as old as it is in Turkey. The states and their institutions are newer still, as are modern economic enterprises. Consequently, the relationship among religion, state, class and culture remains unusually fluid.

This does not mean that the microcosmic, everyday lives of contemporary East Africans are for the most part still conditioned by precolonial ethnic cultures and social solidarities alone, nor is their more self-conscious political behavior. That ethnic *gemeinschaften* remain needs no emphasis, but the new states are not simply arenas for raw ethnic competition and conflict, as news reports might sometimes lead one to believe. For one thing, the precolonial societies of the region were never as discrete as would be suggested by the lines anthropologists are accustomed to draw on "tribal" maps. There were "international" political systems in East Africa before the coming of Arabs and Europeans and there was much cultural interchange. The image of Africa as a stagnant region is now recognized for what it is: a product of Western ignorance and prejudice. The "dark continent" has in fact been the scene of vast population movements, of the rise and fall of countless kingdoms and empires. Everyman, in East Africa as elsewhere, sporadically experienced, and took part in, macrocosmic events reaching beyond the microcosms of his everyday experience. Furthermore, I want to suggest, both his microcosmic and macrocosmic worlds have been profoundly shaped by recent history so that ethnicity is now a different thing from what it was. The cycle of European imperial conquest and penetration, colonial administration, nationalist agitation and independence is by now familiar to the most casual newspaper reader, but the sociocultural residue of these and earlier events is much less well understood.

East Africa (like most of Africa), is, to put the matter in somewhat different terms, a region of "multiple realities" (Schutz 1962:207-59) par excellence. Nation–state and ethnic *gemeinschaft,* trade union and political party, precolonial religion and the newer monotheisms, modern education and the older patterns of socialization: all are "real" in various situations, in varying degrees, and at different points in people's lives. Furthermore, persons born at different times have experienced recent history differently. In many areas, the period of effective colonial administration was relatively brief, so that people who as children experienced the effervescent excitement that came with the achievement of independence had known grandfathers or great–grandfathers whose earliest memories had been of an East Africa into which Europeans were only beginning to penetrate. Understanding the significance of the various realities in the experience of contemporary East Africans is a task requiring open–minded and painstaking study by all the relevant methods and perspectives at the disposal of the social sciences.

Such understanding, one must say, has been ill–served by some of the recent debate among social scientists, not to speak of politicians, over the relative significance of the various kinds of social ties and the methods of studying them. Politicians may be forgiven their obfuscations in such matters, since in the nature of their calling they have other fish to fry. Social scientists who obfuscate what are intrinsically difficult enough problems serve neither social science nor Africa. I have in mind the ill–tempered arguments about the significance, in the African context, of ethnic ties, or what is often called "tribalism." Articulate Africans, understandably, tend to dislike both the word and the phenomenon it is used to denote. The word "tribe," in its classical sense, properly applies to only *some* precolonial African societies, as it does to some pre–Roman European ones.[2] "Tribalism" today usually means "ethnic divisiveness." I shall avoid these words because of *their* divisiveness, but the problem to which they draw attention cannot properly be dodged. African states *do* contain diverse primordial solidarities, as do most other societies, and these solidarities, in Africa as elsewhere, sometimes rise insistently to self–consciousness and become divisive, occasionally threatening the integrity of the states. Fostering the illusion that these phenomena do not exist or may be made to disappear rapidly by ignoring them is both dishonest and unhelpful.

Religious ties are also "real." It is often suggested that Islam and Christianity sit rather lightly on their East African converts — that, as it is often rather crudely put, African Islam and Christianity are "only skin–deep." This view, of course, has a certain plausibility, and even a certain persuasiveness, in two senses: first, it is doubtless true that many East Africans, like many of their predecessors elsewhere in Christendom and the Islamic world, converted more because membership in Christian or Muslim communities offered political, educational or economic advantages than out of a coercive sense of salvation in Christ or of submission to God's Holy Law; and second, while there is along the East African coast an ancient Islamic culture, most East African Muslims and all East African Christians, whatever the depth of their *personal* commitment, are the granchildren or great–grandchildren of non–Muslims and non–Christians, so that the time depth of their cultures' and societies' engagement with the "universal" faiths is shallow and its working–out very incomplete. Furthermore, probably a majority of the East African population is still neither Christian nor Muslim in any sense.

2. Lewis and Short (1879): "*tribus*: a division of the people, a tribe . . . some . . . the same as the names of gentes (descent groups)."

But it is deeply important that the very large majority of the politically more active part of the population *are* Muslims or Christians in some sense of that a very pervasive, and probably irreversible, process of syncretism between the montheistic faiths and indigenous cultures has been set in motion. The new religions and the secular culture which accompanied them have substantially influenced the structures of everyday life, providing linguistic and cultural media for action and experience which now cross-cut and moderate ethnic solidarities. In all this, the old African religions, which the census takers have taken to lumping together under the often misleading rubric "animism," cannot, of course, be ignored. I do not mean to ignore them, but of that and the problem of "syncretism" more later.

Of course there are other interethnic influences in the East African situation besides religion. In particular there is the element of "common interest," economic and political, which in varying degrees and ways unites numbers of East Africans across ethnic lines. But the pursuit of common interest does not take place in a cultural vacuum. Organizational structures — political parties, trade unions, economic enterprises and bureaucracies — are no more than that; they are social formats for organizing persons toward common goals. They require a measure of common language and common understanding about ends, means and the structure of the situation in which they operate. Both commonalities of precolonial culture[3] and common experience of the colonial and postcolonial situations contribute to the meaning worlds of purposive organizations; but, I believe, so also do the monotheistic religions and those

3. Despite linguistic diversity and political atomism, sub-saharan African societies have much in common. Few Africanists would dispute this, but synthesizing the vast quantity of historical and ethnographic material now available will be the work of many decades.

aspects of secular Middle Eastern and European culture which arrived with them, or in their train.

The colonial East Africa which I first visited in 1950 was a rather placid place. Despite ethnic and religious heterogeneity and despite great economic and political inequality, daily life was not, for the most part, characterized by fractiousness or by a simple, sullen acquiescence to imperial authority. Even in the cities, where Europeans, Indians and Africans of many ethnic groups rubbed shoulders and where, consequently, there was a good deal of friction and tension, interpersonal relations were reasonably civil. In the countryside, most Africans lived in ethnically rather homogeneous communities governed by their own local authorities in accordance with the British policy of "indirect rule." To be sure, this relative calm rested, ultimately, upon British imperial power and upon the framework of colonial administrative and judicial institutions through which it contained incipient conflict. There was, of course, occasional dissent from these arrangements and, more rarely, rebellion against them, as there had been from the beginning of their establishment, but relatively few persons were yet aware that imperial legitimacy was beginning to crumble, in their own minds and in those of their fellows.

Among better-educated Africans, however, the curve of dissent had, by 1950, begun to rise perceptibly. This was so particularly in Kenya, the only one of the East African territories in which European settlement had been substantial enough to impose a pattern of social and economic life reminiscent of southern Africa, with all the resentments this sort of situation stimulates among Africans (see, for example, Kariuki 1963; Rosberg and Nottingham 1966). In Uganda and Tanganyika, Europeans were for the most part officials and missionaries, while Indians were merchants. In Kenya, Europeans were also land-owning farmers, and their numbers were much greater. Furthermore, the more politically aware Africans throughout the region knew, during the late 1940s, that India had achieved independence and that in West Africa well-organized nationalist movements were pressing toward the same end. Nevertheless, on the part of the vast majority of East Africans at the beginning of the 1950s (again, the Kikuyu of the Kenya highlands were the exception), the British *imperium* seemed to be regarded not merely with acquiescence but as possessing a rather substantial degree of legitimacy.[4] Within this framework, incivility arising from ethnic or religious conflict or from conflicts of interest remained remarkably rare.

A good index is provided by the effectiveness of the courts of law. East Africans greatly admire the litigious and judicial skills and value tribunals in which such skills may be deployed to achieve the just settlement of disputes. Precolonial legal institutions varied from hierarchies of formally-constituted courts in the more centralized polities, in which legal concepts were manipulated in a quite "legalistic" manner, to the more *ad hoc* tribunals of the less centralized, more "segmentary" polities in which mediation, arbitration and the restoration of the *status quo ante* played a larger role. British administrators, no doubt reflecting their own common law tradition, gave great attention to these institutions, reserving to them substan-

---

4. The day King George VI died, the retired Musoga chief with whom I was staying — a man who had had his difficulties with the British administration and who was regarded by them as a fairly subversive character — declared a day of mourning and summoned his people to his compound. He spent the afternoon solemnly showing them pictures and reading to them from a volume on the lives of British sovereigns. He seemed most concerned to assure them that it was acceptable for a woman to succeed — a custom unknown to Basoga in their own country. Few were old enough to remember Victoria. Here as elsewhere, the myth of "the king's wicked servants" played a role in the maintenance of legitimacy. There was great affection and respect for the British sovereign; wrongs were attributed to lesser beings.

tial "customary law" jurisdiction while reforming their procedures. This policy was of course more readily accepted by the peoples who already possessed more differentiated legal institutions, but in general, throughout the colonial period, both the reformed customary courts and the new magistrates' and appeals courts were regarded as legitimate and prestigious institutions and as modern legal training became accessible, Africans increasingly sought it. A regard for the rule of law united all communities to a remarkable degree (see, for example, Fallers 1969).

In what follows, I shall give a brief account of the historical development of the pattern of cross-cutting ties and solidarities and then describe some of its vicissitudes during the past twenty years — years which have seen the colonial territories of 1950 become nation-states. My conclusion will be that, despite some incidents of marked — even violent — conflict, the pattern has held and that it has contributed substantially to such stability and civility as East African society has enjoyed through a period of rapid change. That is to say, in a situation of this sort — a situation in which a large number of formerly autonomous and diverse societies were, within the space of less than a century, thrown together into ethnically quite arbitrary aggregations, ruled and deeply influenced by external powers and then set free as sovereign nation-states — the question to be asked is not why these states have experienced so much difficulty in maintaining unity but rather why they have experienced so little. The pattern of cross-cutting social ties and cultural worlds, I suggest, is at least partly responsible.

The East African coast has been under Near Eastern influence, principally from the Hadramaut and the Persian Gulf, since before the beginning of the Islamic era. Muslim traders and settlers simply entered a pattern of Red Sea, Persian Gulf and Indian Ocean commerce which had been in existence for some hundreds of years. In medieval times, there developed a Muslim–Bantu language and culture stretching from the Juba River in Somalia to the Rovuma, which forms the Tanzania–Mozambique border. Its linguistic expression was Swahili, the language of the *sawahil* (Arabic: "coasts"), a Bantu language heavily infiltrated with Arabic and Persian words and written in Arabic letters. Its social organizational expression was the trading town, linking the hinterland with all the ports of the Indian Ocean basin and beyond through trade in slaves, gold, ivory and such oriental exotica as rhino horn, in exchange for cloth, and later, firearms. It was this complex which Ibn Batutta encountered in the course of his grand tour of the then Islamic world.

This Swahili society and culture remained, true to its name, a coastal phenomenon until the nineteenth century. Meanwhile, the Portuguese appeared on the coast at the beginning of the sixteenth century and for a time dominated it, along with much of the Indian Ocean. In the seventeenth century, there was a resurgence of Muslim power in the form of the Arabs of Oman and Muscat and for a time there ensued a three–way struggle among Portuguese, Omani Arabs and the old Muslim rulers of the coastal towns. Finally, in the late eighteenth century, the Omani Arabs established their predominance, with Zanzibar as their headquarters. As the British and Germans appeared on the scene in force in the nineteenth century, Zanzibar, under the Busaidi dynasty, exercised a loose *imperium* over the whole coast north of the Rovuma and had established Swahili–speaking slave– and ivory–trading communities up country across present–day Tanzania and into what was to become the Congo (now Zaire). All this, then, collapsed in the late nineteenth century under British and German pressure: what is now mainland Tanzania became German East Africa, Kenya became British

East Africa and the Zanzibar islands themselves became a British protectorate.

Swahili culture, however, remained and spread under British and German administration (German East Africa became British Tanganyika after the First World War). The coasts were the bases from which European dominion developed, and hence Swahili was their lingua franca, as it had been that of the Arabs before them. Islamic law and Muslim judges were recognized. This was particularly the case in Zanzibar and also in Tanganyika, where the Swahili complex had thrust inland before the Europeans arrived. Swahili, now latinized, became the language of administration and, partially, of education. It even became, in many cases, the language of Christianity, as well as of Islam, for the Christian missionaries, too, began on the coasts. Although they converted few coastal people (apart from up–country slaves freed by the British authorities), since those native to the coast were already Muslim, their first translations of the Bible, the catechism and prayer book were into Swahili. With independence, Swahili became the national language of Tanganyika, and then of Tanzania, when Zanzibar was joined to it. In the Zanzibar islands themselves, as in the rest of the coastal zone, essentially the whole population were Arab or African Muslims.

A deeply Arabized and Islamicized language thus became the national language of Tanzania, a country of whose population only a small minority were Muslims. In part, of course, this was made possible by the fact that precolonial Tanganyika was politically, ethnically and linguistically even more heterogeneous and atomistic than the other East African territories; none of the ethnic languages was extensive enough to compete with Swahili. But the continuing spread of coastal culture was more than linguistic. The coastal communities and their up–country outliers, such as Tabora, provided a pattern of cosmopolitan town life that continued to draw into itself recruits from up–country peoples. This effect is perhaps most concretely illustrated in patterns of housing and urban growth. Urban life was not indigenous to the East African interior, most of whose peoples favored dispersed settlement, and in Uganda and interior Kenya, where Swahili communities never fully established themselves, urban growth took place almost entirely under European and Indian auspices. The typical result was what one geographer has called the "alien town" (Larimore 1959): a township or municipality built in concrete and kiln–dried brick according to rather high standards established by British planning officers. Africans lived in sanitary, but rather bleak "housing estates" or "labor lines" or else in completely unplanned suburban villages in village–type houses, outside the township or municipality to which they commuted to work. Africans regard these urban complexes as the places of foreigners, where they themselves go reluctantly and only in response to rather narrowly economic motivations. In such coastal cities as Zanzibar city, Mombasa and Dar es Salaam, however, the indigenous urban pattern was recognized by European officials. There one finds a distinctive Swahili house built of mud, wattle and coral rag and roofed with palm frond, designed to front on a town street, and professional builders who specialize in their construction (see Leslie 1963). British officers in charge of these communities laid out streets and later provided electric lines, but otherwise allowed growth to proceed in response to demand. The result was that, although the coastal towns contained at least as high a proportion of Europeans and Indians as Kampala and Nairobi, all spoke Swahili and Africans on the coast could identify with the city and consider it theirs to a far greater extent. This complex has continued to absorb thousands of up–country people.

Thus in Tanzania Swahili culture has become to an important degree a basis for national culture. A nationalist movement and government, led by a pious Roman Catholic, expresses its ideals in Bantuized Arabic Muslim words and Bantu syntax: the republic is *jamhuri*; "freedom" is *uhuru*; African socialism is *ujamaa*; President Nyerere himself is "Muwalimu" — *'alim* (scholar–teacher) to the nation.

To the north, in Kenya and Uganda, the pattern of development was rather different. Although the Kenya coast is of course part of the Swahili complex, with a thousand years of Islamic civilization behind it, the up–country penetration of the complex was far less marked than was the case in Tanganyika. For reasons which are not entirely clear, but which apparently have to do with more formidable opposition from up–country peoples, Swahili traders approached the Lake Victoria area, not directly, along a straight path from the coast, but rather from the south through Tanganyika; they arrived only shortly before the Europeans, and then not in very great force. In this region, ethnic blocs are generally larger and more cohesive, especially to the north and west of the lake, where for some centuries there had existed large kingdoms with highly centralized administrative organizations, the largest of which were Buganda and Bunyoro. Even the politically more decentralized societies of the area represent large ethnic blocs (Kikuyu, Luo and Luhya, for example). Swahili traders arrived not long before the middle of the nineteenth century. Kabaka Mutesa I, the king of Buganda, became a Muslim and it seems likely that, if Europeans had not intervened, these up–country states would have developed into inland counterparts of the coastal sultanates. Kabaka Mutesa learned to read and write Swahili and kept the fast of Ramadan for ten successive years. But then, in the 1870s, Protestant and Roman Catholic missionaries arrived, soon backed by British empire–builders. What might have become a Muslim–Bantu civilization developed instead into a Christian–Bantu one.

The story of the evanglization of the lakes region is a fascinating and intricate one, but I must summarize. Both Roman Catholic and Anglican missionary effort, and then British empire–building, chose to focus upon the Buganda kingdom, which had emerged during the previous century as the dominant power of the region around the northern lakes. There followed, in the 1870s–80s, a period of intense religious competition, which centered upon the palace and particularly upon the young men who served in the royal page corps. These were boys who had been sent to the palace by their chiefly families to learn the ways of palace politics while serving the king, hoping to be noticed and chosen for office in the royal administration. Ganda society was characterized by high social mobility; while it contained strong clans and lineages whose internal organization was based upon patrilineal descent, the administrative structure at this period was largely free from direct hereditary recruitment; the kings had managed to assert control over appointment to most offices, and therefore the hierarchy was largely open to men of talent. The palace, and especially the page corps, was the crucial recruiting ground, and hence whichever faith succeeded in attracting these young men would, in the natural course of palace politics, come to dominate the country (Fallers 1964:Ch. 1, 2, 3, 6).

The details of what followed are exceedingly complex, as only palace politics, accompanied by religious proselytizing and empire–building, can be. Suffice it to say that in the competition for influence over successive kings, who were gradually becoming aware of the magnitude of the outside forces then impinging upon them, the monotheists won out

over the "pagans," the Christians over the Muslims, and the
Anglicans over the Roman Catholics in a setting reminiscent of
the conversion of Europe, the crusades and the wars of religion
all rolled into one. Young Buganda Christians became succes-
sively martyrs (whose sacrifice was recently memorialized in a
moving oratorio in the Ganda musical idiom, performed in
Rome on the occasion of their canonization); then leaders of a
church militant and finally a Christian, landowning gentry led
by Knights of the British Empire and of the Papacy — all this
under a British protectorate which treated Buganda as the
dominant center of a wider Uganda with greater internal
autonomy than the other Bantu kingdoms and the non-Bantu
districts. Some of these men acted as the agents of British administration, extending a kind of neo-traditional Ganda form
of centralized, bureaucratic political structure, and in some
cases the Luganda language, to neighboring peoples — both to
Bantu kingdoms, whose own institutions were already similar,
and to non-Bantu peoples whose polities had been smaller and
less centralized. Others became Anglican and Roman Catholic
catechists and priests, carrying Christianity to neighboring
peoples.

The churches were rapidly Africanized in personnel and indigenized in their relationship to local society and culture. The
White Fathers of Algiers, who carried on much of the Roman
Catholic effort, soon became mostly black fathers, as did their
Anglican counterparts. With the churches came schools whose
facilities were eagerly sought by members of these relatively
open societies in which Western education had now replaced
palace service as the recruiting ground for talent. By no means
did all the people of Uganda become Christians, particularly
outside Buganda, but it is safe to say that essentially all their
leaders (except for those of the Muslim remnant) did so. It can
also be said that during the first half of the present century such
incipient national culture as Uganda possessed was the product

of the churches and their schools. This, however, was not expressed in a common language, as was the Swahili–Muslim culture of the coast and Tanganyika. Swahili itself was spoken in this region largely as a market language. The elite lingua franca was English. While Luganda spread some distance outside its native borders, and while the Bantu languages of southern Uganda were in any case similar enough to make intercommunication easy, the languages of the large ethnic blocs of the Nilotic north belonged to an entirely different family. Administration, worship and primary education thus came to be carried on in some six or eight ethnic languages. But Anglican synods and Roman Catholic sodalities, and the schools associated with both churches (for a long time located mainly in Buganda) brought together elite members of all ethnic groups. The leadership of African society in Uganda in the inter–war period was firmly Christian and heavily Baganda.

In all this, the universalizing role of Roman Catholicism was greater than that of Protestantism. Under British rule, the Anglican church tended to be the church of establishment (not legally; there is a good deal of controversy about what sort of influence the Protectorate government actually exerted in these matters, but it seems no accident that the kings of all the Bantu kingdoms of the south came to be Anglican). The Anglican churches became the "national" churches of the kingdoms, while the Catholics, perhaps in part because of their oppositional position, tended to adopt a more interethnic, all–Uganda orientation.

I shall not stop to describe the corresponding developments in Kenya. In many ways, the pattern there is intermediate between those of Uganda and Tanzania with respect to the interaction of religion, culture and the state; in other ways it is unique. It is unique in the dominant position which, for a time,

European settlers occupied in its affairs. It is intermediate in that the Swahili component is stronger than in Uganda, weaker than in Tanganyika. As in Uganda, there are large ethnic blocs (e.g., Kikuyu, Luhya and Luo), which have made the growth of a Swahili–based national culture more difficult than in Tanganyika. The pattern of Christian missionizing, however, is more similar to Tanganyika; whereas in Uganda Anglicans and Roman Catholics have largely shared the field between them, in Kenya there are also Presbyterians, Methodists and Quakers, as well as — perhaps partly as a result of this fragmentation of mission effort and of the more abrasive racial situation resulting from European settlement — a flourescence of breakaway nativistic and syncretistic sects. In Tanganyika, the German period had left a substantial Lutheran community as well.

Here it is necessary to say a further word about the problem of syncretism and the depth of East African Islam and Christianity. The relationship between the universalistic religions and their environing societies and cultures is always problematical, which is indeed what the word "universalistic" means in this context. While the problem by no means presents itself in precisely the same way for Muslims and Christians, they share, and their histories repeatedly illustrate, the problem of relating their radically transcultural appeal to their institutionalization in particular societies and cultures. There is always, for them, the problem of what it is that unites Christian Jew and Greek, Muslim Arab and Persian, and at the same time the problem of speaking to each in an idiom sufficiently familiar to be relevant to the round of daily life and to more macrocosmic events and projects. In their relations with each other and with indigenous East African cultures, the monotheisms have in the past tried *jihad* and crusade in the effort to create integral Christian or Muslim societies and

cultures, but these solutions now seem foreclosed. Both have
interacted with local cultures in a syncretism which is simply
inevitable for such faiths. I must limit myself to one example:
Peter Lienhardt, who has carried out one of our few careful
field work studies in the Swahili area, reports a conversation
among some members of the community of Kilwa, the same
community than Ibn Batutta visited in the fourteenth century.

> Among those present were a Matumbi, a Yao, a reformer of cus-
> tom, a religious shaikh, and a Muslim stranger from Mombasa.
> Both the Matumbi and the Yao have shrines for ancestral spirits,
> and the reformer was criticizing them for this. He announced
> provocatively that to maintain these shrines was forbidden
> (*haramu*) in just the same way as eating pork. The Yao replied that
> his tribe was accustomed to this old traditional way of maintaining
> shrines to ancestors whom they asked to help them in their dif-
> ficulties. The reformer told him: "You are all unbelievers and
> neither full Muslims nor full pagans. You are just giving foreigners
> the opportunity to criticize us." The Yao said that theirs was sim-
> ply a harmless custom; it was just a matter of remembering the
> ancestors and was simply like saying the *fatihah*. [5] The stranger,
> playfully encouraging the controversy, asked why, if this was
> forbidden, the Muslims used a prayer calling by name on those
> who had fought by the Prophet's side at the battle of Badr: Were
> they not all dead people? The religious shaikh announced that
> Muslims read this prayer in order to ask the people it mentioned to
> pray to God for them in accordance with their wishes. The
> Matumbi and the Yao then said that if this was so, surely they had
> the right to ask their ancestors to pray for them. Another Matumbi
> finished off the conversation by saying that praying to the ances-
> tors was effective, but it was still wrong. (Lienhardt 1966:383)

I have heard many analogous conversations among
Baganda and Basoga Anglicans and Roman Catholics,
especially in the context of weddings and funerals — occasions
on which both the ancestors and the monotheistic faith come

---

5. The opening chapter of the Koran.

insistently to mind. The dialogue continues, but it continues in a spirit of reasonable tolerance because a degree of pluralistic civility has been institutionalized in these communities. The dialogue has become a routine part of everyday life.

Both the colonial and postcolonial situations have nurtured this village–level civility. Particularly is this so in the relations among Christian churches and between Christianity and Islam. However much British administrators may have favored Christians over Muslims and Anglicans over Catholics during the period of empire–building, governmental policies during the colonial period proper were favorable to interreligious civility. Roman Catholic and Anglican archbishops and Muslim ulema were always present on great public occasions in a pattern rather resembling the "interfaith" public rituals of the United States. In educational policy, all groups were aided by public funds, with special care being given to assist the Muslims, who had fewer resources to draw upon from the outside; latterly the philanthropy of the Aga Khan has also greatly helped to overcome Muslim educational backwardness and defensiveness in East Africa. More recently, Christian ecumenism has become a real factor. While the universalistic religions have become deeply indigenized in local communities, these communities are also in effective touch with wider tendencies in their world communions. Zanzibar and other cities of the coast have been centers of Muslim learning, open to the various Islamic orders and schools of law, as well as to the thought of such "modernists" as Muhammad Abdu.[6] Many ordinary East African Muslims make the pilgrimage to Mecca, where they encounter all the varied

6. In an excellent study, now in press, Abdul Hamid el Zein describes the Bantu–Muslim island community of Lamu, north of Mombasa. The community has elaborated its own version of Islamic tradition and is also in contact with the Muslim centers of the Middle East and the Indian Ocean.

currents in contemporary Islam. Roman Catholic and
Anglican prelates have lately taken to making expansive ges-
tures of brotherhood toward each other and toward Islam. It is
significant that Cardinal Rugambwa of Tanzania and the
African bishops of the Anglican church have been leaders in
the *aggiornamento* efforts of their respective international
communions, suggesting that the impulse to religious civility
arises from the pluralistic East African setting as much as it im-
pinges upon it from the outside. The East African situation
thus represents a kind of collapsing of religious history as know
by Western peoples. The universalistic religions there today
face, among the more highly educated, the challenge of
secularism at the same time as they remain in contact, at the
village level, with large numbers of persons still committed in
varying degrees to the older ethnic religions. The eras of initial
conversion, establishment, reform, secular skepticism and
ecumenism coexist.

The East African societies, while they are economically
backward and poor, and while their new polities remain
somewhat tentative, are not traditionalist in the sense of having
a deep attachment to ways of thinking and acting felt to be continuous with the distant past. It is not, of course, that such at-
tachments are absent, but rather that within any of the states
they are so numerous and diverse as to be unusable for the
definition of a common *national* tradition. East Africans have
engrafted themselves onto several varieties of Christian and
Muslim tradition in their nineteenth century forms — forms to
which modern technology and education were already integral
for the Christians and have since become so for the Muslims —
forms in which the "war between science and religion," at any
rate in its cruder versions, had become a dead issue, so that one
accepted Christ (or the Holy Law) together with, for example,
modern medicine. One, or one's children, also absorbed in

school some knowledge of modern world history, its conflicts and its ideologies: nationalism, egalitarianism and a utilitarian attitude toward material progress, both individual and social. Consequently, as Kenyans, Ugandans and Tanzanians, East Africans are strikingly modern men at the same time that, as Kikuyu, Baganda and Luo, they may continue to harbor strong "traditionalist" sentiments. The colonial experience served to collapse their histories and to set them on new courses. If the struggle for independence was, with the possible exception of the Mau Mau episode in Kenya, a rather mild affair compared with the nation–forming revolutions that shook the Western world in the nineteenth century and some non–Western societies in the twentieth, the colonial experience as a whole provided a new beginning somewhat analogous to revolution.

Within these truly new nations, ethnic and religious solidarities become elements in a novel sort of pluralism. All of them still contain remote areas in which the eight or nine decades of missionizing and colonial administration passed with relatively little effect — I am thinking of areas of central Tanzania and of northern Uganda and Kenya — but all of them also contain areas, including rural, peasant village areas, in which mosque and church congregations have been present long enough to be fully part of social life. These areas tend to be the areas of greatest agricultural development and are most closely and actively in touch with central governments. They, together with the towns (which of course are even more markedly pluralistic, both ethnically and religiously), have an importance in the national societies which is quite out of proportion to the numbers of people contained in them. They participate more fully and supply a greater proportion of leaders to national institutions. Their pluralism, furthermore, is of a sort in which even a person's kinsmen may well not be coreligionists and may not belong to the same political party, or even the same state. During the colonial period, the three incipient states shared a number of common services — post and telegraph, customs, railways and harbors among others — and throughout the period the question of some sort of closer federation among them was debated. Both interterritorial migration in search of employment and the accidents of boundary demarcation have resulted in situations illustrated by that of the Luo, who are represented by substantial numbers in all three states.

Thus, the possibility of "over-participation" (Shils 1957) in ethnic *gemeinschaft,* religion or state tends to be moderated by participation in the others. This does not, of course, mean that incivility in the form of over-participation in one or another of these ties is held perfectly in check. Each of the states has experienced periods of marked — even violent — incivility, instances of which I shall describe. Nor do I mean to suggest that pluralistic civility is the only quality required by the new East African states. It does not, by itself, provide the organizational and material resources for the economic development which East Africans desperately want and need. But civility is a crucial resource, especially for peoples who aspire, as East Africans have aspired, to develop in a reasonably free and open political atmosphere. Their success, thus far, has been very imperfect, but their difficulties have been enormous, since the very effort to develop, and to redistribute the fruits of development, tends to exacerbate ethnic rivalries inherited from the past and to weaken the interpersonal bonds of civility. Two series of episodes may serve to illustrate the way in which macrocosmic events break into and arise out of the microcosmic lives of men and women, become crucial life experiences, both personal and collective, and elicit actions which, although understandable in terms of past experience, produce results which may properly be called "revolutionary." One took place in the coastal zone, in Zanzibar; the other in interior East Africa, in Uganda.

The Zanzibar islands (Zanzibar, Pemba, Tumbatu) are part of — indeed until colonial times were the political center of — the coastal zone, where Islam and the Swahili culture are most fully in conjunction. Some ninety percent of the population are Sunni Muslims. This does not mean that there is no diversity of primordial loyalties. I have already mentioned the waves of settlement that have washed over the coast and the islands; in Zanzibar there are the "indigenous" Swahili-speaking peoples, the Hadimu, Pemba and Tumbatu, each of whom had their own political institutions before the Omani Arab settlements of the eighteenth and nineteenth centuries. These are often collectively referred to as "Shirazi" since many of them trace the Middle Eastern side of their heritage to a migration from Shiraz in Iran. Similar Swahili-speaking Muslim groups exist on the mainland coast. There are also the Omani Arabs, who upon arrival became political suzerains, later sovereigns and eventually, in the nineteenth century, as Zanzibar became the source of most of the world's cloves, the Omani Arabs became plantation landlords, in the process intermarrying, adopting Swahili and often losing Arabic. Finally, there are up-country Africans who have come as slaves and, more recently, free migrant workers; they also adopt Islam and Swahili, but some, especially the more recent migrants, retain a sense of difference from the Shirazi and of course from the Arabs. These primordial "groups" are, however, far from discrete, as is clear from the radically shifting proportions represented by each in successive censuses (Bartlett 1936; Zanzibar Protectorate 1924, 1931, 1953, 1960). In a situation in which there is a shared basic religion and language and in which there has been much intermarriage, the self-identifications given to census-takers

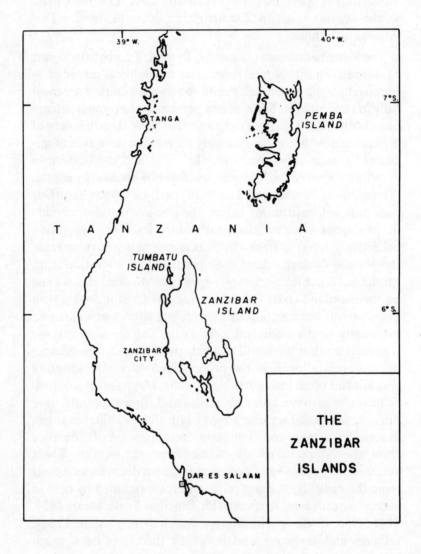

39° W.

40° W.

TANGA

PEMBA
ISLAND

7° S.

T A N Z A N I A

TUMBATU
ISLAND

ZANZIBAR
ISLAND

6° S.

ZANZIBAR
CITY

THE

ZANZIBAR

ISLANDS

DAR ES SALAAM

become expressions of self-chosen primordial loyalties. During the three decades prior to independence, the censuses show a tendency for the "Arab" category to grow markedly and for the remaining, or more "African," population to shift toward self-identification as "Shirazi," "Hadimu," "Pemba" and "Tumbatu," at the expense of the general category "Swahili," which tends to have derogatory connotations of slave origin. During this same period, events in the Middle East, especially the enhanced popularity of pan-Arabism led by Nasser's Egypt, greatly heightened the ethnic self-consciousness of the Arabs. During my visits to Zanzibar in the middle 1950s, it seemed all radios were tuned to Radio Cairo.

During the decade before independence, as party political activity grew, there developed a still greater polarization toward more Arab and more African identification, culminating in the revolution of January 12, 1964, when the Sultan's government was overthrown and Arab landowners expropriated, many being killed, imprisoned or driven into exile. Power was seized by a small, avowedly Marxist, group calling itself the "Umma Party."

Ethnic polarization was far from complete, however, as analysis of both the name and composition of the new revolutionary leadership reveals. The leadership contained both "Africans" and "Arabs" and the term *umma* means "Muslim community," not "the masses," as some writers have translated it (Lofchie 1965:258).[7] It seems likely that, to a population much of which had been Muslim for centuries, the term carried more the connotation of Muslim universalism

7. This otherwise very useful study is marred by an insensitivity to matters Islamic and hence by a tendency to misinterpret the meaning of race and class in an Islamic society. The Arab/African dichotomy certainly exists on the East African coast, but it is thought of more in genealogical than

*(Continued on page 58)*

than of class war. Among the general population, polarization was much greater on Zanzibar Island, where "Africans" were largely plantation or town wage workers, and where many of these were recent immigrants from the mainland, than on Pemba, where "Africans" as well as "Arabs" were independent clove farmers. This economic differentiation appears to have stimulated such ethnic polarization as emerged in the last pre-revolutionary election. The Afro-Shirazi Party, which spoke for "Africans," received slightly more than half the total vote, heavily concentrated on Zanzibar Island; while on Pemba most "Africans" voted for the Zanzibar and Pemba People's Party, which was allied with the Zanzibar Nationalist Party — the "Arab" party. These results served to further heighten political tension. Because of the unbalanced distribution of votes among constituencies, the election gave a majority of parliamentary seats to the Z.P.P.P.-Z.N.P. alliance, despite the Afro-Shirazi majority in the popular vote. The latter felt themselves cheated of victory.

Even so, the revolution which followed seems to have been something of a fluke. While the polarization of primordial sentiments and economic interests was real enough, the actual outbreak of violence was led by an intriguing figure, "Field Marshal" John Okello, a wandering Christian visionary and revolutionary from Uganda. Because of the concentration of

---

phenotypic terms. A person, however dark, who can plausibly (in local terms) claim Arabian descent in the male line is socially an Arab. This is confusing to Americans, whose culture classifies as "Negro" anyone with perceptible African ancestry. Again, economic exploitation is thought of less in the stratigraphic or layer-cake imagery common in Europe and America than as an affront to Islamic egalitarianism. There has, of course, been much exploitation in Islamic societies; the point is that when there is protest against it, that protest tends to be expressed in Islamic terms. The term "*Umma*" — Islamic community — evokes the theme of equality among Muslims, rich and poor. Wealth is legitimate when it is combined with generosity.

police arsenals in one quarter of Zanzibar city — the quarter occupied mainly by mainlanders — he was able to seize the whole armed force of the territory with only a small band of conspirators. When it was over, he was promptly expelled by the new government — not the first self-appointed revolutionary leader to have tipped the delicate balance in a fluid situation nor the first to have been rejected by those who had benefited by his intervention.[8]

Zanzibar then entered the very loose Tanzania union with Tanganyika. One is bound to wonder, though, whether, in the absence of Okello, Islamic universalism might not have held — whether it might not have continued to provide a basis for consensus sufficient to keep ethnic and economic conflicts within more civil bounds.

Events in Uganda may be treated in somewhat greater detail, not because they are inherently more complex, but because more of my knowledge of them is from first-hand experience and I am able to make use of others' observations with greater confidence.

Politics in Uganda between the Second World War and independence, which came in 1962, also exhibited a crystallization of primordial self-consciousness and the formation of ethnic blocs. Here, however, the critical revolution-precipitating event occurred more than a decade before its final consummation and its agent was not a radical soldier of fortune, but rather a carelessly loquacious British

8. Okello has given his account of these events in his *Revolution in Zanzibar* (1967). He appends the "official" account published by the government that expelled him — an account that ignores his role — and remarks that he was warned that he would be rejected because Muslim Africans and Arabs would combine against an interloper. If Okello's account doubtless exaggerates the part he played, the "official" account is clearly more inaccurate and self-serving in treating him as a "non-person." See Lofchie (1965:274-77).

colonial secretary. It may be described in terms of two acts, separated by a twelve–year interlude.

During the late 1940s and early 1950s, the Kingdom of Buganda, which had dominated Uganda under the British Protectorate,[9] appeared to observers to be moving toward greater internal democracy and a more accommodating relationship with the other peoples of the territory. Agricultural cooperatives tinged with populist political ideology grew up and these seemed to be directed as much against the chiefly oligarchy as against the Protectorate regime. Kabaka Mutesa II, the Muganda king, was becoming unpopular with his people as a vain young playboy–autocrat and captive of the British. When the first really plausible nationalist movement aimed at securing independence was formed in 1952, it was inevitably dominated by Baganda, since Buganda remained by far the most developed part of the country, both economically and educationally; but the Uganda National Congress, as the new party was called, soon formed branches in other districts and its executive contained a number of non–Baganda. The movement toward an all–Uganda national consciousness was strengthened by the arrival from Britain of a new, liberal governor, who believed in rapid advance toward self–government and also, as a corollary to this, in a unitary Uganda state, of which Buganda would form an integral part.

Then, in the summer of 1953, the then Colonial Secretary, Oliver Lyttleton, in the course of an after–dinner speech in Nairobi, revived the notion of a "closer union" among the three British East African territories. This was the issue which Kabaka Daudi Cwa, Mutesa's father (whom I quoted at the

9. The Agreement of 1900 between Britain and Buganda gave the latter much more internal autonomy than was accorded other areas of the Protectorate. See Low and Pratt (1960).

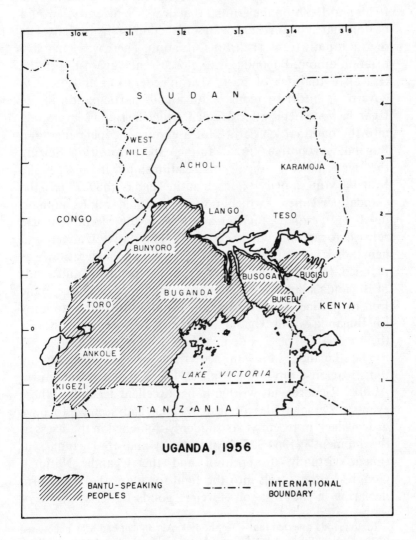

UGANDA, 1956

BANTU-SPEAKING PEOPLES     ―·―·― INTERNATIONAL BOUNDARY

beginning of this chapter), had successfully fought during the 1920s and 1930s on the ground that any such federation would be dominated by the European settler community in Kenya; its revival rapidly transformed the situation. There was a massive reaction among Baganda, who closed ranks against both the revival of the idea of East African federation and the new governor's effort to increase Buganda's participation in the Uganda–wide Legislative Council, which he saw as developing into the national legislature for a unitary independent state. Baganda saw both as threats to their special position. Seizing the opportunity to repair his relationship with his people, Kabaka Mutesa placed himself at the head of the *Lukiiko,* the Ganda parliament, which now represented public opinion much more solidly than at any time in the recent past. He refused to appoint members to the Legislative Council and demanded assurances that no East African federation was planned. He also demanded a date for independence and a shift of Buganda's link with Britain from the Colonial Office to the Foreign Office — in effect a concession of further autonomy for Buganda within Uganda.[10] When he refused to withdraw these demands, he was deported to Britain.

The Baganda were stunned, then puzzled, then angrily united against any compromise. The Kabaka must return. Audrey Richards has written in her excellent account of these events: "Personal ties of fealty which had seemed to have grown slack in recent years suddenly tightened in the stress of the moment" (1964:323). Antiroyalist and all–Uganda sentiment virtually disappeared and the Uganda National Congress threw itself into the fight for the Kabaka's return, declaring a boycott on foreign goods. The symbols of

10. Baganda asserted that since the 1900 Agreement had been negotiated by the Foreign Office, the take–over by the Colonial Office a few years later had been improper all along.

traditional culture were revived on a large scale in a society very largely Christian or Muslim and with a relatively high level of literacy and education. Men grew beards — a traditional sign of mourning — and women staged protest meetings demanding the return of "our husband."[11] The cults of the traditional divinities were revived. Money and gifts were collected to be sent to the Kabaka and delegations flew back and forth between Kampala and London organizing the campaign for his return. A lawsuit was brought by members of the *Lukiiko* testing the legality of the deportation.[12] British officials found it difficult to carry out their duties, though there was relatively little violence.[13] Impressed by the magnitude and persistence of the reaction, the British government appointed a distinguished historian to mediate the issues between a committee appointed by the *Lukiiko* and the Protectorate government. Ultimately, a compromise was reached and after two years in exile the Kabaka returned. Under the terms of the new agreement, the Baganda agreed to participate in the Legislative Council, but the internal autonomy of the Kabaka's government was substantially increased and East African federation was quietly buried. In theory, the Kabaka himself was to become a "constitutional monarch"; in practice, because of the circumstances of his return, he was virtually all-powerful in Ganda affairs.

11. In nineteenth-century Buganda the Kabaka might claim any Muganda woman, married or unmarried, as a wife. Mutesa II remarks somewhat delicately in his memoirs that "the nature of my relationship with the Baganda involves me even more closely with women than with men." Mutesa II (1967:147).

12. The court found the deportation to be an unjusticiable "act of state," but also found that if it *had* been justiciable, the government's case contained technical flaws. This was enough for the Baganda to claim victory.

13. Interestingly, while administrative (political) officers were finding great difficulty securing cooperation, I observed agricultural officers working quite normally with Baganda farmers.

The effect of the two years' experience of humiliation, reaction and victory (as Baganda saw it) was a great strengthening of collective solidarity and self–esteem. Audrey Richards describes Mutesa's return:

> The celebrations . . . proved to be a large–scale representation of the political structure of the traditional monarchy at the height of its power at the end of the nineteenth century . . . . The Kabaka was displayed as the head of the administration of Buganda, greeted at the airport by the ministers and chiefs. After his triumphal drive . . . to Kampala, the seat of his capital, his first visit was to the Great *Lukiiko,* where his chiefs in official robes greeted him on their knees to the thudding of the royal drums which had been silent for two years. Delegations from each county and sub–county had brought, or would bring, presents . . . . His Highness was also greeted as *Ssaabataka,* head of all clans. The clan officers had redoubled their activities during the mounting enthusiasm for traditional things . . . . Each clan and sub–clan had collected money for the Kabaka in his exile. Their leaders came in deputation with presents after his return. The day after the signing of the new Agreement was fixed for the first of the clan football matches which had been such a feature of Buganda's sporting life and which had come to an end after the deportation. The new Buganda government building, opened in splendor shortly afterwards, had bas–relief models of clan totems in colored terra cotta round the entrance doors. (1964:331)

Thus ended the first act, with Buganda triumphant in its relations with the Protectorate government, but poised for another struggle with that government's African successor after independence, for although Buganda remained the most advanced part of the forthcoming nation, and its ecological center, its people were still a minority of the population and its legitimacy as the *moral* center, such as it had been, had been eroded by its intense self–preoccupation during and after the deportation. Earlier, Buganda had been the object of envy; now envy increasingly turned into resentment. "At first we thought we would be held back by our more backward neighbors," Mutesa wrote in his memoirs; "later we feared that a combination of the rest of the country might from motives of self-interest seek to destroy us. Both fears proved well-founded" (Mutesa II 1967:149).

While Baganda were consolidating behind their returned king, other ethnic groups in Uganda were catching up educationally and in their sense of themselves as citizens of a future independent Uganda. Inevitably, this took the form of a decreasing tolerance for Ganda dominance. David Parkin's excellent study provides a microcosmic view of interethnic relations in two public housing estates in Kampala during the period just before and after independence (Parkin 1969). These estates, reflecting the working population of the city, were highly heterogeneous, their 1,468 households being distributed among more than eighteen ethnic groups. Luo migrants from Kenya were more numerous than Baganda. Other prominent groups included Nilotic- and Sudanic-speaking peoples from northern Uganda and Bantu from the other Uganda kingdoms and from the Kenya-Uganda borderland. Parkin's sketch of the Ganda candidate for councillor for Kampala East ward, which included the two estates, in the 1962 municipal elections reflects the heightening of ethnic sentiment as political self-consciousness increased:

> The Ganda candidate . . . was a sub-county chief and was said to be of the royal clan . . . . He contrasted strikingly with the other candidates in standing aloof from the proceedings. He did attend meetings and rallies, dressed in his *kanzu* and jacket, the traditional dress for Ganda men, but a younger Ganda, dressed in lounge suit and speaking impeccable English and Swahili, as well as Luganda, addressed the meetings on his behalf. Ganda residents explained that they expected a Ganda chief to behave in this aloof manner. They were not at all affronted that he did not personally address the meeting, though others, notably the Kenyans and

66                                                CHAPTER TWO

northern Ugandans, complained about this and also that a man,
whatever his rank, who lived twenty miles distant could hardly be
expected to represent the ward properly . . . he . . . had not associated with residents of the estates on a personal basis before the
election. (Parkin 1969:34)[14]

Thus Buganda's very position as ecological center represented a kind of time bomb in its relations with non–Ganda,
since Kampala, the center of the center so to speak, contained a
growing and increasingly alienated non–Ganda element.

This municipal election and the approach of the following
one in 1964 also provided the setting for the heightening of
another sort of consciousness — the consciousness of national
boundaries. During the colonial period, East Africans had
moved freely among the three territories with little sense of
crossing boundaries, but with the approach of independence,
Kenyans began to realize that they would soon be dis-
franchised in Uganda. Statements by some Uganda officials
suggested that they might lose their jobs as well, since times
were hard and there were demands for preference for Ugandan
workers. Many of the leaders therefore broke their ties with
their kinsmen in Uganda and returned to Kenya to participate
in electoral politics there, although a large community of
Kenyans remained in Uganda as expatriates. The
Kenya-Uganda border had taken on a solidity in people's
minds that it had previously lacked (Parkin 1969:44-51).

It remains only to describe the party political struggle
through which the second act of the revolution in Buganda's
relations with its neighbors was played out. As independence
approached, three parties had emerged: (1) The Uganda
Peoples' Congress, an outgrowth of the old Uganda National

14. Under the existing electoral law, non–resident property owners could
run for office in the ward.

Congress, minus its Ganda leadership and having a strongly all–Uganda appeal; (2) the Democratic Party, also all–Uganda in orientation but identified particularly with the Roman Catholic church; and (3) a royalist party, the *Kabaka Yekka* (literally "the Kabaka alone"), a Ganda ethnic party pledged to preserve Buganda's autonomy through a federal relationship with the rest of Uganda. While the complex series of negotiations with the British government proceeded, an election for the National Assembly (which had replaced the Legislative Council) was held. Since the issue of Buganda's relationship to the new state remained unresolved, the K.Y. boycotted the election and relatively few — mainly Roman Catholics — voted in Buganda where, virtually unopposed by either K.Y. or U.P.C. (whose strength lay in other areas), the D.P. won all the seats. With additional seats from other areas, the D.P. accumulated enough to form the interim government; its leader, a Muganda Roman Catholic, led the delegation to the final constitutional conference in London in 1961. The D.P. victory, produced by a religious split among Baganda, created great bitterness among K.Y. supporters, but at the conference, where the Kabaka's representatives were also present, the Baganda achieved their desired federal status. In the final pre–independence election, the U.P.C. and the K.Y. formed a winning alliance. The U.P.C. leader, Mr. Milton Obote, a Lango from the north, became Prime Minister of an independent Uganda and subsequently Kabaka Mutesa was elected President.

This unlikely coalition lasted two years, after which relations between Buganda and the central government steadily deteriorated, while Prime Minister Obote, in an atmosphere of financial scandal and military intrigue, moved increasingly toward personal rule. Then, on May 24, 1966, the military forces of the central government were launched against the

Kabaka's palace. Many Baganda were killed or imprisoned, although the Kabaka himself escaped to die in exile in England. The monarchy was abolished. From the point of view of most Baganda, jealous to the end of their autonomy and loyal to their king, it was a wholly unjustified attack by an external force; from the standpoint of Obote and those loyal to him, it was revolution against an entrenched and haughty oligarchy.

Since the two revolutions (1964, 1966), there have been no elections in Zanzibar or Uganda, although the authoritarian rule fastened upon both countries has not remained undisturbed. Prime Minister Obote has been overthrown by General Amin, his chosen instrument for personal control of the Uganda army, and in Zanzibar, President Abeid Karume, who achieved power through Okello's coup, is dead by an assassin's bullet.

What meaning, for the social anthropology of the nation–state in East Africa, may we find in all these tragic events? In both cases there were great inequalities of wealth and power which might plausibly be represented by leaders as ethnic inequalities, even though there were many poor Arabs in Zanzibar and many poor Baganda in Uganda. I have heard otherwise humane persons, well–informed about both countries, describe the revolutions and their authoritarian aftermaths as "inevitable under the circumstances"; I find this interpretation unacceptable. My more general grounds for rejecting historical inevitability will be presented in my last lecture. Here I simply restate my argument that throughout East Africa there exists a basis for pluralistic civility in the pattern of cross–cutting ties and solidarities. Neither Uganda nor Zanzibar need necessarily have fallen into uncivil disorder if the persons in positions of leadership and authority had acted in time to avert it. The colonial power waited too long in reducing inequalities and thus in preventing the politicization of ethnic loyalties in the new states, launched so hopefully into sovereignty with liberal democratic constitutions. Political leaders, inexperienced in the arts of electoral and parliamentary politics, yielded too easily to the temptation to manipulate primordial loyalties and economic grievances for personal political advantage. And then there were "accidents" of personality — Okello and Colonial Secretary Oliver Lyttleton. To say all this is not to sermonize at men now dead or fallen into obscurity. It is simply to recognize that history is not made up only of the sorts of economic, ecological and sociocultural structures and patterns that social anthropologists and other social scientists may discern. History is also made by men and groups of men, themselves conceptualizing and choosing among the courses of action offered by their situation.

Revolutionary experiences have the capacity to transform both common culture and personal identity. And yet one suspects that in the microcosms of East African life the bases for more civil politics remain. East Africans remain Muslims, Protestants and Roman Catholics, as well as Baganda, Arabs and Kikuyu. Some economic progress has been made and the occupational structure has become increasingly differentiated. Authoritarian rule has not had the capacity to become totalitarian, even where it has aspired to become such. If the future of civil politics seems highly uncertain — indeed, at this writing, quite unpromising — it is also not foreclosed.

# three

# TURKEY:
# NATION-STATE OUT
# OF POLYGLOT EMPIRE

. . . ethnic communities lose their identity in the
course of history by becoming part of a larger religious or political community and of a larger civilization which is common to all ethnic units united
within it. They emerge once again as nations by res-
cuing their character from the bonds of these three
larger unities. They undergo important changes
during their life in these three universal communities. It is because of this that when a nation is
reborn it ceases to be the same old ethnic
community.

ZIYA GÖKALP, 1917

Ziya Gökalp was the first professor of sociology at the
University of İstanbul and he was an engaged intellectual —
one whose formulation of the problem of Turkish nationhood
has been highly influential both in the ideological life of his
country and in foreign observers' views of it. He was also an
*academic* intellectual, a true social scientist; he maintained,
through a momentous period in Turkey's history, a certain distance from day-to-day political events and a tension with
politicians which kept him apart from the inner circle of those
who were remaking the nation and which left him somewhat
under appreciated by later generations. His cool, analytic essays are remarkably penetrating. They show, I believe, that had
he lived in less chaotic circumstances he might have contributed significantly to that turn-of-the-century burst of

71

social scientific creativity that I referred to in the first chapter as the "macrosociological synthesis," for he was remarkably in touch with the mainstream of European thought even while situated on Europe's periphery. In particular, he might have contributed a comparative perspective from within Islamic tradition, for he was well-educated in the orthodox classics and the literature of Islamic mysticism as well as that of European sociology.

My subject, however, is not an unjustly neglected scholar — although that is one well worth pursuing — but rather the peculiarly Turkish experience with the nation-state. In 1917, when Gökalp wrote the passage I have cited (1959:132), his own political community was at the point of dissolution. The Ottoman empire, following more than six centuries of first rapid expansion and then gradual decline, had fatefully allied itself with the Central Powers in the First World War and was about to participate in their defeat and humiliation. Ottoman armies had won significant victories against both British and Russian forces and one hitherto rather obscure officer — Col. Mustafa Kemal (later Atatürk) — had so distinguished himself at Gallipoli that he was able to rally his countrymen to resistance and then reconstruction. But although the Ottoman imperial house survived by a few years (if only in a formal sense) those of Austria, Germany and Russia, its non-Turkish territories, apart from Kurdistan, were gone. In fact more Turks now lived under other sovereignties — Greek, Yugoslav, Bulgarian, Iranian, and above all Soviet Russian — than inhabited the rump of empire that remained in Anatolia and eastern Thrace. Indeed, the victor of Gallipoli and those he rallied to him were required to fight on for three more years after the general armistice of 1918 to salvage even that much, since the Allied Powers had agreed in secret protocols to distribute much of the remaining territory among themselves.

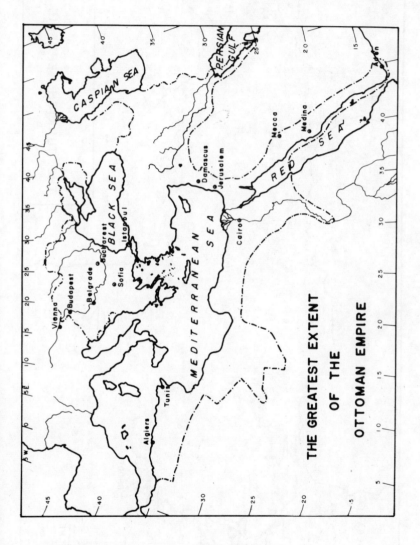

THE GREATEST EXTENT
OF THE
OTTOMAN EMPIRE

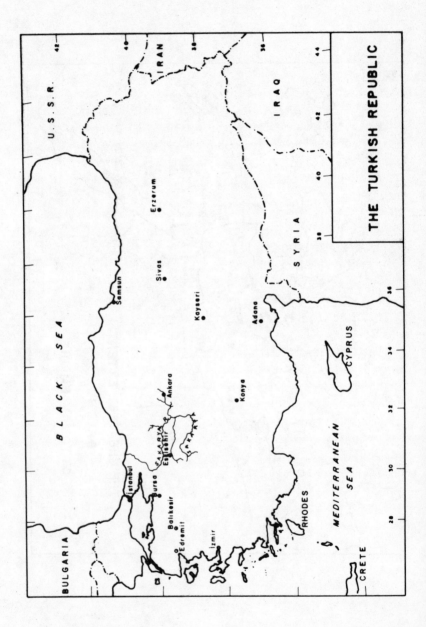

THE TURKISH REPUBLIC

Within the space of less than a decade the Turks passed from the status of faltering imperial overlords to that of nationalist freedom–fighters. Their fight was principally against the Greek army of invasion since Britain, France and Italy had had enough war and rapidly lost interest, while the Russians had become, for the time being, too preoccupied with their own internal struggles to concern themselves with those of their ancient enemies astride the Bosphorous. The forces led by Atatürk waged a successful "War of Independence" against both the Greek invaders and the "Army of the Caliphate" which the government of the Sultan–Caliph, having capitulated to the Allies, had turned against the nationalists. The most developed regions of the country were left decimated and in ruins; the successful expulsion of the invader, however, provided the new regime with gifted leadership and an heroic national myth. The "sick man of Europe" had been reborn a bright and vigorous, if somewhat scrawny, child (Robinson 1963:Ch.3).

So much, for the moment, for the macroscopic view. The work of local chroniclers and historians (Balcioğlu 1937; Yetkin 1939, 1957[1]) enables us to view all this as well from the standpoint of the people of a provincial city who, while Ziya Gökalp was brooding over the problems of nation, state and civilization in İstanbul, were sensing the reverberations of the guns of Gallipoli in the boilers and chimneys of their olive oil presses and mustering the last of their draftable manpower for dispatch to the front. Like the Ottoman empire, their city had had a long and checkered career and was now facing deep crisis.

Edremit is an old city — much older than the empire — having been known as Pedasus, Adramis, Adramyttium and

1. A chronicle extracted from the last work is given in Appendix A to this chapter.

perhaps other names as well by its various Lydian, Persian, Greek and Latin rulers. Situated at the head of a mountain–rimmed gulf on the Aegean coast of Asia Minor, opposite the island of Mytilene (Lesbos), its population was largely Byzantine Greek when, in the year 1231, Yusuf Sinan, son of a magistrate and leader of a band of holy warriors (*gazis*), seized it on behalf of Islam and the Seljuk Turkish sultanate of Rum.[2] It appears to have been a place of some size and substance then,[3] since Yusuf Sinan caused to be erected there a small, but rather finely–constructed, mosque in the late Seljuk style, in whose courtyard his mortal remains lie buried. A saint by virtue of his services to Islam, his tomb is even today bespattered with the fresh drippings of votive candles placed there by women whose marriages have proved barren or whose sons or brothers have gone off to military service to be exposed not, of course, to the dangers of war — for Turkey is at peace — but to the more elusive ones of distant cities. A notice erected by the orthodox religious authorities warns against the excessive veneration of the saint as bordering on polytheism, but fresh drippings appear none the less.[4]

It is said that Yusuf Sinan built his "Leaden Mosque" (*Kurşunlu Cami*) — so-called from the material of its domed roof — on the edge of the city, foreseeing that it would in future become the center of a much larger community. Indeed he foresaw correctly: the city as it then existed, surrounding the

2. During the twelfth and thirteenth centuries the town was more than once raided and sacked by Turkmen tribes, then retaken and fortified by Byzantine forces. After its incorporation into the Seljuk sultanate it became part of the Danişmend emirate of Karesi. The area was incorporated into the Ottoman empire in 1341. See Yetkin (1957:6); Vryonis (1971).

3. Vryonis (1971), citing Anna Comnena, frequently speaks of Byzantine Adramyttium and quotes Ostragorsky as listing it among "the more important towns" of Asia Minor.

4. Here, as elsewhere in Turkey, othodoxy continually stresses strict monotheism, but "polytheism" in the form of saint cults is a common heresy.

"lower market," remained largely Greek until the early 1900s, while the area around and beyond the Leaden Mosque became a new "upper market," around which new residential quarters, largely Turkish in population, grew up. The histories of these quarters mirror that of the empire: some, during the centuries of Ottoman expansion, were settled by retired soldiers and westward migrants from as far away as Kazakistan; others, as the empire shrank, became the homes of returning Turkish refugees from the Crimea and the Balkans. As they have lived out their everyday, microcosmic lives as citizens of the provincial city, the people have been rather more aware than most provincial Turks of macrocosmic events and have participated more actively in those events.

Today, turning off the İstanbul–İzmir road, one enters the town along a wide, paved street flanked by the excellently–kept municipal park and gardens. Edremit is one of Turkey's largest and most modern county seats, with a wholly Turkish–Muslim population of some 30,000 merchants, artisans, olive growers, wage workers and small commercial and industrial entrepreneurs and their families. The town is progressive and prosperous, and rather cosmopolitan in outlook; located as it is on the narrow coastal strip, separated by mountains from interior Anatolia, it has always communicated more easily with İstanbul to the north and İzmir to the south — and with Eastern Europe — than with its own hinterland. Today fleets of motor busses facilitate this traffic. Indeed, my wife and I chose to do fieldwork on social change there in part because of the region's economic, cultural and demographic "modernity." Its fertility rate is in the European range and we guessed that people who plan their families also plan other aspects of their lives. Edremit and its attached villages have always been rich by Turkish provincial standards. "Olive oil," its boosters say, "flows down one main street, honey down the other." At present the economy has begun to diversify from an almost total dependence upon olive cultivation and processing to new crops and products. A tractor–trailer factory now under construction, which will employ some three hundred men, as well as a number of smaller establishments manufacturing electric welders, farm machinery and the like, is introducing a new social category: the industrial worker.[5]

Present–day Edremit also contains local branches of all the principal national institutions: government offices of all kinds, schools, political party branches, more than a dozen mosques, eight banks, two hospitals, wholesale and retail outlets for the state monopolies, philanthropic organizations and an army training base. While artisan craftsmen still pursue their work in iron, brass, copper, leather and cloth in open bazaar workshops, the main streets of the central business district are now lined with clothing, dry goods, hardware, grocery, stationery and other shops of the "modern" sort (that is, with plate–glass display windows on either side of the entrance) and there are even two small department stores. A series of vigorous mayors and city councils have transformed much of the town with new streets, sewers, and water and electric services. The quaint narrow, crooked, cobbled lanes overhung with the latticed dormers of mud brick and half–timber houses are being replaced by wide, paved streets lined with cement–block houses and flats; the community is secure enough, now, for some of its members to worry about the aesthetic costs of urban renewal. There is a sense of well–being about the place. God, most people seem to feel, has smiled upon Atatürk's republic, and especially upon this corner of it.

There are, of course, other moods. The people of Edremit read the newspapers and listen to the radio; they are suf-

5. An outline of the occupational structure of Edremit is given in Appendix B to this chapter.

ficiently into the modern world to share its general restlessness
and many of them fret about Turkey's own very real political
and economic problems. Many of the townspeople are also
olive growers and a son of the North American prairie
recognizes among them the universal farmers' dissatisfactions:
if the crop is good, prices are, naturally, too low and the rain
always falls at the wrong time. But to a visitor familiar with the
recent history of Turkey and that of its Aegean region, the
scene seems strikingly placid.

During the First World War, however, the outlook must
have seemed bleak indeed, and worse was to come. When the
men and women of Edremit heard the guns of Gallipoli, they
must have thought of sons and fathers, husbands and brothers,
fighting there — men whom Col. Mustafa Kemal[6] was order-
ing "not merely to fight but to die," as legend has it, to prevent
the British forces from consolidating their beachhead, and
thereby opening the straits and the Black Sea to Allied naval
vessels and shipping to aid the Russians. The straits were held,
but at fearful cost to communities like Edremit: by 1915 there
had already been three call-ups of men from the community
and by 1917 all but three of the city's reserve officers were dead.
There can have been few men of any age or status left to draft,
for unlike the countries of Western Europe, August, 1914, had
found Turkey already bled of able-bodied men by decades of
war. There had been war with Russia in 1877, with Greece in
1897, with Italy in Tripoli in 1911, and then, in rapid succession, the two Balkan wars of 1912 and 1913, as well as the
smoldering conflict in the Yemen (which I have heard a distinguished Turkish writer call "the Ottomans' Vietnam"). All
this shows quite plainly in present-day population pyramids,
both local and national: the higher age-cohorts are pitifully

6. For an account of Atatürk's life and military campaigns, see Lord
Kinross (1964).

truncated. Middle–aged people today speak of themselves as "the fatherless generation" (see Appendix C to this chapter).

Apart from light shelling of its seaside suburbs by Allied gunboats, however, the city itself remained outside the actual theater of military operations during the First World War. Men were conscripted, supplies were requisitioned, there were extra taxes, and, of course, there were shortages: when kerosene became unavailable, the people burned olive oil in their lamps, as their ancestors had done. The dead were mourned and commemorated in the customary recitations of the Turkish *mevlûd* — Süleyman Celebi's poem on the life of the Prophet. But life in the city went on and there was even progress. The first cinema was opened by the municipality and under a vigorous and popular new county governor, Hamdi Bey, construction of the first sewer system was undertaken and a new school and library established. As in much of western Anatolia, the truly "dark days," as townspeople now recall them, began after the armistice.

On May 19, 1919, Mustafa Kemal, now a Pasha or general officer, having tricked the government in İstanbul, then under Allied occupation, into sending him to Anatolia to disarm the troops there, instead landed from a steamer at Samsun on the Black Sea coast and proceeded to raise a movement of national resistance against the terms of the peace imposed by the Allies — terms which the Ottoman government had accepted. Nine days later, Edremit received a telegram from the Pasha inviting its people to join his movement. Four days earlier, with Allied support, Greek forces had landed at İzmir and were preparing to move inland to annex Asia Minor. In Edremit, as in many other towns, protest demonstrations were held and a chapter of the "Society for the Rejection of Annexation" was organized with the tacit support of Governor Hamdi Bey, who shortly found himself sacked by the authorities in İstanbul. His succes-

sor harrassed the nationalists and Hamdi Bey himself took to
the mountains to organize irregulars in support of Mustafa
Kemal Pasha's new national government, now established in
Ankara. The notables of the small neighboring county seat of
Burhaniye expressed their defiance by firing off a telegram to
İstanbul declaring their county's secession from "the
government of the Sublime Porte." Within a few months,
however, the entire Aegean coast had fallen under Greek occupation.

Again, as during the First World War, the decisive battles of
the War of Independence were fought elsewhere. In the
interior, on the Anatolian plateau, where Kemal was able to
raise and equip regular forces from men and equipment not yet
demobilized, fighting rearguard actions against the Greek advance until, at the great bend of the Sakarya river, only fifty
miles from Ankara, he was able to stand and turn the tide
against his over-extended enemy and then begin the westward
drive that forced the Greeks back to their ships at İzmir.

Edremit and its environs were not fought over by regular
forces and thus escaped the effects of the "scorched-earth" tac-
tics adopted by both sides. The communities of the region experienced instead the materially less destructive, but perhaps
socially more demoralizing, consequences of more than two
years' enemy occupation, with its inevitable train of defiance
and repression, collaboration and revenge. Here, as elsewhere,
selective memory creates what the English satirist Dudley
Moore has called an "aftermyth of war." The following, in its
entirety, is the account of "Edremit in the War of
Independence" given in the book prepared by a local teacher to
supplement the history texts supplied by the Ministry of
Education:

> At ten o'clock on January 1, 1920, Edremit, whose brave sons had
> shown great heroism from the rocky slopes of Albania to the firey

wastes of Yemen defending soil that was not ours, was occupied by
the Greeks. On June 6, 1920, our heroes, who had joined the force
organized by Governor Hamdi Bey on May 5, 1919, were forced
by the collapse of the Balikesir and Soma fronts to lay down their
arms. They had fought for 410 days, spilling their blood and giving
their lives. For 797 days Edremit's people remained under enemy
occupation and experienced grave dangers, but on July 9, 1922,
they embraced the returning Turkish columns who were pursuing
the enemy. (Derin 1968:24-25)

Following this passage there appears a photograph bearing
the caption "Republic Square in Edremit, Birthplace of
Heroes."

There *was* much suffering and heroism. There was also a
good deal of settling of personal scores and simple banditry,
encouraged by uncertainty about where authority lay or indeed
ought to lie. As one old man told me, "Every man sat in the
coffee house with a pistol in his lap." For it was only in
retrospect that the fight could be clearly viewed as one between
two nations — Greek and Turkish. Governor Hamdi Bey was
finally captured and executed, not by the Greek army, but by
an irregular force of Turks loyal to the Sultan. Even the
struggle between ethnic Greek and ethnic Turk was in some
measure an internecine one, for the two communities had for
centuries lived together in Asia Minor under a common
government and many of the men who now served the
government of Venizelos in Athens were legally Ottoman subjects who had severed both personal ties and ties of citizenship
to serve the "Great Idea" of restoring Greek ascendancy in Asia
Minor. Similarly, many of Edremit's Muslim people were immigrants from the European provinces, ethnic Turks whose
families had lived for generations in the Balkans and the Greek
islands and had only recently returned as these territories
slipped from Ottoman control. The Ottoman civil and military
services contained a great many such men and both Atatürk

and Governor Hamdi Bey, the local hero, were among them. Nor could the war be viewed simply as one between Muslim and Christian, for while Kemal was now known as "*gazi*" ("warrior for the faith") in Ankara, he and his government lay under the official religious condemnation of the Şehülislam, the chief religious official in İstanbul.

The War of Independence instead became what Atatürk and his followers quite explicitly wished it to be: a crisis of identity in the course of which a new source of authority was legitimated. When first the sultanate (1922) and then the caliphate (1924) were abolished,[7] the ground had been prepared by a bitter conflict in which men and women inexorably, and often against their will, had been forced to choose between ethnic nationalism and loyalty to a theocratic dynasty which for centuries had ruled over Christians and Jews as well as Muslims, over Arabs and Kurds, Albanians and Greeks, Serbs, Bosnians, Bulgarians, Circassians and a dozen other ethnic communities, as well as Turks. In Ziya Gökalp's formulation, in the course of the war the Turks had emerged from Islamic civilization and the Ottoman polity and were now prepared — at least the large majority who opted for, or acquiesced in, Atatürk's Republic were prepared — to give their allegiance to a secular Turkish nation–state patterned after the states of Western Europe.

This process, while in the legal sense consummated by the establishment of the Republic, continues to this day. The great post–war population exchanges through which Turkey and the new states of eastern Europe sought to make themselves

7. The Ottoman sultans claimed the title "caliph" — religious leader of the Islamic world — a world within which in principle religious and political authority were fused. The Ottomans' claim was not universally acknowledged, but it was sufficiently recognized so that a storm of protest broke out in Muslim India and elsewhere when Kemal, in an effort to separate government from religion, abolished the title in Turkey.

ethnically more homogeneous, and which still continue, particularly with Greece and Bulgaria, are perhaps the most obvious manifestation of this process,[8] but they are by no means the most important. The Republic created a new identity, but the effort to confer meaning upon this identity — this Turkish republican citizenship — goes on, since the life of a nation-state is not an event or a static structure; it is an experience and an experiment, a continuing working out of commitments and relationships, a venture in political community.

The first two decades of the Turkish republican venture were dominated by Atatürk's famous reforms. For some twenty-five years he and his Republican People's Party maintained a monopoly of political power — authoritarian, but not totalitarian, a distinction important to preserve in a time when the word "fascist" has come to connote for many people any exercise of authority felt to be unpleasant. In the Europe of the 1930's, which Turkey now set out to emulate, the distinction was crucial. Atatürk and his colleagues were often ruthless and there were brief flirtations with racist ideas — particularly improbable in a nation to whose gene pool nearly the whole of the Old World had contributed, but perhaps an inevitable concomitant of the effort to establish a national identity at that period. In any case, as Bernard Lewis has written, Atatürk's was

> . . . a dictatorship without the uneasy over-the-shoulder glance, the terror of the doorbell, the dark menace of the concentration camp. Force and repression were used to establish and maintain the Republic during the period of revolutionary changes, but no longer . . . Political activity against the regime was banned and newspapers were under strict control, but apart from this talk, and even books and periodicals, were comparatively free. Critics of the

8. Appendix C to this chapter shows the proportion of Edremit's population who were born outside the borders of present-day Turkey.

regime from the humbler classes were left alone; critics among the ruling elite were, in accordance with earlier Ottoman practice, punished with governorships or embassies in remote places. Violence was rare and usually in response to violent opposition. (Lewis 1961:285)

The program of reform to which this monopoly of power was devoted was farreaching: secularization of the state and of public education; suppression of the dervish (*sûfî*) orders which had contributed so much to Turkish culture but which were now distrusted as sources of reaction and revolt; replacement of remaining Islamic law by European codes and adoption of the Western calendar; latinization of the script and a purging of many Arabic and Persian elements from the language; the legal emancipation of women; the establishment of state banks and industries to stimulate economic growth; encouragement of the Western fine arts in place of Middle Eastern ones. The call to prayer from the minaret was now to be in Turkish rather than Arabic, thus separating Turkey from otherwise universal Muslim practice. All this was capped, quite literally, by the famous "hat law" replacing the fez and turban with fedora and peaked cap. If men dressed their heads in a Western manner, Atatürk said, they were more likely to think Western thoughts. *Western* thoughts, mind you, not merely *modern* ones. Unlike Japan and the excolonial new states of the post–World War II period, Turkey under Atatürk sought to join the West, not merely to compete with it at the game of "modernity" (Lewis 1961:395-436). Naturally there was opposition. One man in Edremit, outraged by it all, declared that he would obey the Gazi's orders and throw away his fez, but he would never sully his head with the infidel hat. He went bare-headed in every kind of weather for the rest of his life.[9]

9. Elsewhere there was more serious opposition, notably a revolt led by the Nakşıbendi order in eastern Anatolia.

Was it "reform" or was it "revolution"? The ambiguity is embedded in the language, for *devrim* means both. It carries the sense of an "over-turning;" the changes just listed, however, are most frequently spoken of collectively with the plural form, *devrimler,* not as constituting a single *devrim.* Indeed, the continuity of personnel from the old regime to the new renders the connotations of the English "revolution," in the sense of "social revolution," quite inappropriate. The Republic inherited from the shattered empire little of material value beyond land and water, but the human legacy — a largely intact army and civil service — was crucial. There was also a very substantial continuity of ideas and political-cultural style. Ziya Gökalp, who provided the most important intellectual complement to Atatürk's political genius, was only the latest in a long series of intellectual advocates of Westernizing reform, just as Atatürk himself stood in a line of reforming rulers running back at least to Mahmud II at the beginning of the nineteenth century. There had been the Tanzimat reforms in law and administration in the 1840s and 1850s as well as the constitutional experiments of the latter decades of the nineteenth century (Lewis 1961:75-126; Feroz 1969). Some present-day Turkish revisionist historians are even rehabilitating Sultan Abdul Hamid as a reformer, especially in education (Lewis 1961:178; Kuran 1967). Atatürk's regime, then, was in significant respects an extrapolation from existing precedents.

Nor, looking ahead, did it turn out to represent as clean a break with the more traditional elements of Ottoman life as the exaggerated rhetoric of the regime and its foreign celebrants might suggest. The Republican People's Party called itself "populist" (*halkcı*) to express its aspiration to eliminate the Ottoman political and cultural gap between the elite and the people and Atatürk himself spoke admiringly of democracy. He even experimented — twice, and briefly — with parliamen-

tary opposition, since there were those among his prominent
supporters for whom political competition along
liberal–democratic lines was a touchstone of legitimate reform.
During his lifetime, however, and for a decade thereafter, he
and his successors maintained the posture of instructors for a
*future* democracy. Many in the party favor such a posture to
this day, making it possible for some members of a new
political generation to charge them with constituting a "new
*ulema*" (religious authorities) issuing from on high
positivist-secularist *fetwas* (authoritative opinions) instead of
Islamic ones, but equally out of touch with popular culture.

Even the place of religion itself remained ambiguous.
Atatürk and his immediate successors were without doubt con-
vinced secularists intent upon severely limiting the place of
Islam in Turkish life. But Islam is not the sort of faith that can
be simply disestablished. In Islam, state and religion are, in
principle, fused. Islam was not "the religion of the state" in the
sense that Christianity in its various forms was in Europe.
Rather it was, and is (in principle) quite literally the polity at
prayer. Islam *is* the Holy Law, a complete guide to life in all its
aspects delivered by God to Mohammed in the Arabic
language. The Kuran is God encodified, rather as Jesus is God
incarnated. There are, of course, many complexities here; even
so, the conviction remained (and remains to this day) in Turkey
that a state whose citizens are Muslims cannot be simply in-
different to a religion the very meaning of whose name is "submission" to a law-giving God. Whether because they
themselves, despite their skepticism, were still deeply conditioned by this view of things or because they self–consciously
feared to tamper too much with matters so fundamental to
their people's lives, the secularism produced by the Kemalists
was a very Islamic kind of secularism. Despite the removal of
all reference to Islam from the constitution, the Turkish state,

through a directorate of religious affairs, remained responsible for the upkeep of mosques and the remuneration of religious professionals. Although in every legal respect Christians and Jews now shared a common citizenship, being a *real* Turk socially and culturally still meant being a Muslim Turk. In the eyes of most people in Edremit, it means being a Sunni, or orthodox, Muslim; even the minority of dissenting Alevi Muslims do not qualify.[10]

During the one-party period of the 1930s and 1940s, the Edremit community participated, possibly not always whole-heartedly, in the new order of things. The president of the local Party branch served as mayor. A "People's House" *(Halk Evi)* was established — a cultural center for the propagation of the new, more Western and secular style of life and thought (and what, for the most part, amounted to the same thing, the doctrines of the Party). In a mild form of *gleichschaltung,* voluntary associations were regulated by the state. A city plan was drafted. There was mixed "ballroom" *(balo)* dancing and drinking — in a community which had always interpreted Islam as sanctioning the strict separation of the sexes in public as a means of guarding female purity and male honor. Among the "enlightened" *(aydın)* families of the city, the dress of women as well as of men emulated that displayed in European magazines. The religion of the mosque was not suppressed (though that of the local dervish orders was), but observance of the fasting month of Ramadan was discouraged and indeed any marked display of piety was out of style. A local publication described the mourning for Atatürk, who died in 1938, in extravagantly secular terms (Yetkin 1939:205-12). Its frontispiece bore a photograph of his wartime deputy and successor, İsmet İnönü, "The foundation of our

10. The popular Sunni attitude toward Alevis is in this respect reminiscent of that of Protestants toward Roman Catholics in the United States.

being, great chief of the nation and President of the Republic."
For some members of the community this period would be
remembered as the glorious zenith of secular reform; for
others, although still venerating Atatürk as the savior of the
nation, the period would be recalled as a time of moral laxity
and infidelity.

Then, during the late 1940s, the Kemalist tutelary state
began to relax its grip.[11] The economic development
stimulated by state investment during the 1930s and by external trade during the Second World War had resulted in a
more differentiated society. Under the empire, most en-
trepreneurial activity had been foreign, or in the hands of
ethnic minorities. By the 1940s, however, a class of native
Turkish entrepreneurs had grown up; these men were now
secure enough to be irritated by the statism which had
produced them. Industrial workers were becoming more
numerous and more assertive; farmers and peasants were an-
noyed by taxes and by the state control of agricultural
marketing, of necessity tightened during the war when a large
army had been kept in a state of mobilization. Intellectuals,
even within the ranks of the ruling party, began to demand
greater freedom. Finally, the international atmosphere at the
end of the war (which Turkey had entered on the Allied side in
time to participate in the founding of the United Nations) encouraged a greater openness. An opposition group was formed
within the ruling party and in 1950, in what surely must be one
of the twentieth century's most unusual events, free elections
were held. The opposition, now organized as the Democrat
Party, won a large majority and the Republican People's
Party, with İnönü at its head, gracefully yielded power and
passed over to parliamentary opposition.

11. The best account of this period is that of Karpat (1959).

Turkey's twenty years of liberal democracy have not been untroubled. The Democrat administration under Adnan Menderes, which held power from 1950 to 1960, encouraged private investment and undertook extensive public investment, especially in roads, electric power and food processing industries. Energies were released, especially in rural areas, which had lain dormant under one-party rule. Indeed, there was much material progress.[12]

In Edremit, Democrats campaigned in the surrounding mountain villages, often receiving an enthusiastic response from villagers whose participation in the nation had previously been limited to a passive role of "objects of administration." A vigorous new Democrat mayor was elected and a new city hall, market and bus station were built. The area became a Democrat stronghold.

However, Menderes' slipshod management of the economy ultimately produced runaway inflation and when his opposition became more vociferous and appeared to be gaining strength, he took advantage of the Kemalist constitution (designed for one-party rule) to suppress his critics. A certain relaxation of the rigid secularism had been in progress since the early 1940s, partly because party competition required greater concessions to public sentiment, which had never fully accepted some of the more stringent secularizing measures. In the eyes of many, however, particularly in the civil service, the army and the universities, Menderes had yielded too much to what they saw as "religious reaction."

These dissatisfactions came together in May, 1960, when a group of army officers, with substantial public support, seized power. The Democrat party was banned and many of its

12. J.S. Szyliowicz (1966) gives an excellent account of this period in villages in another region of Anatolia.

leaders were tried before a special court on Yassıada Island. Menderes and two of his ministers were executed.

The army, however, hastened to return the country to democratic, civilian rule (Weiker 1963; İpekçi and Coşar 1965; Erer 1965). A new constitution with more safeguards against authoritarianism was adopted by plebiscite, elections were held and the new parliament convened only eighteen months after the military intervention. The leading parties were now the Republican People's Party and the Justice Party — the heir to the disbanded Democrat Party, but under new leadership. There were two short–lived coalition governments headed by İnönü, in which various small parties played a role. Then in 1965, when general elections were held, the Justice Party, now under the leadership of Süleyman Demirel, took office with an absolute majority — a majority to which Edremit contributed. A similar result emerged from the general elections of 1969. Under these conditions the economy has revived, following a sluggish period in the aftermath of the military intervention, and the gross national product has shown a growth rate in recent years of six or seven percent. Meanwhile the military remain in the wings as "guardians of the constitution" (Özbudun 1966).

Has Turkey, then become a liberal democratic nation–state? In the history of societies, of course, there are no final destinations, only journeys in one direction or another. Commentators on Turkish society are fond of characterizing its recent experience in terms of great forces in collision. In particular, it is often suggested by both Turkish and foreign writers that an irreconcilable conflict exists between two ideologized conceptions of the Turkish identity: one Islamic and traditional, the other secular and progressive (Gallagher 1966). The Democrat and Justice Parties are often linked with the first tendency, the Republican People's Party with the second. The implication is that such profound ideological division, by exacerbating political competition and eroding civility, makes the long-range prospects for Turkish democracy unpromising.

In search of such light as a social anthropologist can throw on such questions, let me turn back, now, to the microcosmic perspective — to the social life of the provincial city and to the way in which national affairs manifest themselves in the experience of its people. The *kulturkampf* is there, without doubt, but it bears little resemblance to the struggle between hypostacized religion and secularism so commonly invoked in the literature on Turkey.

Cultures and subcultures are not disembodied forces. They shape and are created by the experience of men and women who hold them as they engage, cooperatively or competitively, in projects of social action. Religions and ideologies, to be sure, have internal logics of their own. A Muslim believes that God delivered a law to man through Muhammad, once and for all time and in some detail, a law governing the behavior not merely of individuals but also of societies. He does not and cannot see what a Christian so easily formulates as the relationship between religion and state in the same light as does the Christian who believes instead that God incarnated himself sacrifically in an exemplary man who summoned other men to follow him in living under whatever Caesar might be in charge at the time. And since the two faiths, like the great religious traditions elsewhere in the world, have interacted so profoundly with the other aspects of culture over the centuries, this difference applies not only to the self-consciously pious but to most others as well.

Secular reformist ideology, though less differentiated and articulated because it is newer, also has a compelling logic, especially where, as in Turkey, it, like religion, draws upon earlier themes in the national life. As I have noted, Atatürk had precursors in his role of tutor to the Turks in the new ways. For at least a century and a half, Turkish leaders and thinkers had been grappling quite explicitly with the problems of technological and social-organizational reform, especially in response to increasing Western ascendancy.

Located as they were, the Ottomans were a European, as well as a Muslim, Middle Eastern power and the problem of their relationship to Europe (and latterly America) could be viewed in either of two ways: 1) in terms of the *expansion* or *defense* of the House of Islam, if necessary by techniques borrowed from the adversary; or 2) as a fuller embrace of things European in order to *become European,* although remaining Muslim. This problem has engaged the best energies of generations and it remains today a central feature of the Turkish cultural system. Turks simply cannot avoid — or so, at least, most of them believe — an ever deepening engagement with Euro-American culture in its various forms. Socialism, free enterprise and state capitalism: these and other formulae for material progress have been thrust upon Turkey as a result of this deepening involvement. As a result, "secular reform" is inevitably cast in one or another of these Western molds.

Finally, there is ethnic nationalism. "How fortunate," Atatürk told his people, "to be able to say 'I am a Turk!'" They have believed him, or at least have desperately wanted to believe him. But there is a problem of what, precisely, this should mean for a people who have taken their language from central Asia, their religion from the Arabs, their educational system from France, their taste in clothing from Italy, and whose form of government is an amalgam of elements drawn from a wide variety of European and American sources. Atatürk's effort to invoke an ancient central Asian greatness as a basis for Turkish identity contained a grain of truth, but that truth proved too remote to seize and to guide the contemporary imagination, and in any case Atatürk's own political sagacity recoiled from the irredentist implications of *too* close an identification with the Turks of the Soviet Union and Iran. Perhaps the principal reason for the markedly sacred aura that still surrounds the person of Atatürk is that at their moment of supreme crisis he provided the people of eastern Thrace and Anatolia not with a full-blown self-redefinition but rather with the opportunity to develop one. He provided the leadership to enable them *to endure within those boundaries* — a spatial frame within which the cultural content of Turkishness might be progressively worked out.

The creation of that content out of the themes and issues I have mentioned is still very much in progress, and not only in the minds and words of political leaders and intellectuals, although such persons of course exercise a cultural influence disproportionate to their numbers. The problem of Turkish identity also arises, less clearly and more sporadically, in the microcosmic lives of the people of Edremit and others like them.

Such provincial citizens, too, are influential beyond their numbers, for the provincial city plays an important role as a meeting point and mediator between outward-reaching national culture, institutions and processes on the one hand, and, on the other, the increasingly self-assertive agricultural village majority, activated by two decades of improved communication, economic development and political participation. Not everyone in the city, of course, participates in religion and secular ideology equally and in the same way in the microcosmic settings that make up the round of everyday life. While all the themes I have mentioned touch most citizens in some manner, persons located differently in the social structure typically experience and make use of them differently; the city as a whole experiences them differently at various points in the daily, weekly and yearly cycles. Extraordinary events within or beyond the city bring to overt expression cultural commitments which ordinarily lie dormant, and which have developed unself-consciously over the years.

Islam and secular reformism: each has its professional spokesmen. Insofar as the *kulturkampf* may be said to be institutionalized, it rests in the continuing, though publicly muted, tension between the men of religion — the *hocas* — and the school teachers, especially the secondary school teachers. These latter are the city's principal modernist intellectuals: *münevverler* or *aydınlar* — "the enlightened." In the metropolitan centers, where there is greater sociocultural differentiation, the tension is more explicit. In the provincial towns, where persons of different social types exist in numbers too small to form subculturally insulated groups, the tension is held in check by cross-cutting personal ties.

Organized religion is not monopolized by the *hocas*. Women especially, since they are welcome in the mosques only on holy days, carry on their religious lives in groups gathered in private homes. (The house is in any case the woman's domain, which she controls almost to the exclusion of her husband, while the male domain is the public space of the town, the streets, shops and coffee-houses.) Some men probably take part in dervish rituals, although these are still illegal. Still, the *public* exposition of Islam is concentrated in the hands of the *hocas* of the town's fifteen mosques and in those of the mufti, the chief religious official for the county, and his assistants.

The teachers play a similar role with respect to secular modernism. Again, theirs is not a monopoly. In general, all civil servants of the central government, including the officers at the army training base, are thought of (and think of themselves) as bearers of a more modern and enlightened way of life. The officers' club in particular, by making its facilities available for wedding and circumcision celebrations, proselytizes for a more modern, Western and secular style of sociability. But the ideological commitments of the officers and civil servants are moderated by the technical task requirements of their occupational roles, while the teachers are full time bearers of enlightenment with direct access to children in their formative years.

Each school has, or ought to have, an "Atatürk corner," a kind of secularist shrine containing Atatürk memorabilia — photographs, passages from speeches and the ubiquitous plaster bust. One day each year, on the anniversary of the death of "*büyük Atamız*" ("our master teacher"), this cult is publicly celebrated. It begins with a ceremony in the grounds of the secondary school, timed to coincide with the moment of the leader's death in 1938. Here, and in cities, towns and villages all over Turkey, people stand in silence, whether in special gatherings or at work in shops and fields. Traffic comes to a halt; tools are downed. There are no prayers, however, no recitation of the *mevlûd* with which the dead are otherwise universally mourned and commemorated. Instead there are fiercely patriotic speeches and poems by teachers and students and choral recitations of Atatürk's testament to Turkish youth reminding them of their duty to the Republic. The mufti is present but only as an invited guest. The assembled crowd then walks to Republic Square, where wreaths of flowers are placed around the statue of Atatürk standing in a frock coat. The occasion is entirely "uncontaminated," as many teachers — and doubtless the Gazi himself — would say by "religious superstition."

The *hocas* have many more public occasions on which to expound their message. Each Friday, at mid-day prayers, sermons are delivered at the principal mosques. During Ramadan, the month of fasting, instruction is given each evening, as it is on each of the holy days of the Muslim year: the birth, conception and ascension of the prophet, the feast of the sacrifice, the revelation of the Kuran and the annual day of moral accounting. In addition, there are short summer courses in reading the Kuran, especially for the young. Turkish Islam is very moralistic. Relatively few appear to observe strictly the entire daily round of five ritual prayers which enact in word and bodily movement the believer's submission to God. On the other hand, the moral content of submission in the form of a rather puritanical code of personal conduct and public responsibility is constantly reiterated in the mosques and on the streets. While the *kadis* who once administered the Holy Law as the law of the land are long gone, the *hocas,* and especially the mufti, are directed by the legislation providing for their appointment and remuneration to "teach the public faith and worship" and to "guide the public in increasing its religious knowledge" (*Turkish Government Organization Manual* 1966:100). This perforce means teaching the Holy Law insofar as it is not in conflict with Republican legislation. Disestablishment in Turkey has consisted in rendering Islam voluntary while providing it with public support.

The *hocas* and the teachers thus offer competing contents to fill the concept of Turkishness. The teachers offer modern secular learning, heavily salted with nationalist piety. The *hocas* offer an ancient faith which, although it acknowledges the Republic (much can be overlooked, after all, in a regime which saved the community from the infidel), is one whose moral code is at some points rather sharply at variance with that expounded and exemplified by most teachers and civil servants.

It is perhaps with respect to the role of women that the *kulturkampf* bears most closely on the personal lives of Edremit's citizens. However tenuous its scriptural basis (Levy

1957:124-34), the *hocas* expound a version of Islam which requires obsessive concern with protecting the chastity of girls and the fidelity of women by segregation of the sexes and adherence to a strict code of female dress and demeanor. Atatürk removed the veil, but he could not remove the enveloping clothing, the sexual segregation and the elaborated meaning complexes which support them. The emancipation of women, however, remains a central plank in the reformist platform. Men and women may not worship together, but they are educated together, beginning with the primary years, and many of the teachers are militantly liberated women. There are also many, and increasing, opportunities for educated women in the occupational structure, both locally and in the nation at large. The *hocas'* views on these and other matters of personal conduct still receive somewhat greater support from the community. This support is being eroded, however, by both the cultural influence of the "enlightened" within the town — the local officers' club, for example, holds dances and serves drinks to both sexes — and the ever-increasing involvement of Edremit's people in the life of the great cities of Turkey, and those of western Europe, where large numbers now go to work for varying periods.

Thus, in the round of everyday life the people of Edremit experience events which bring to self-consciousness a realization that their way of life involves a compromise — or rather a complex series of compromises, for various persons and groups within the town have worked out different solutions — among the various cultural strands which their history has given them. Very striking to a foreign observer is the degree to which the international implications of the *kulturkampf* are on the minds of ordinary people. There is an undercurrent of anxiety — stimulated, of course, by the foreign anthropologists' presence — concerning whether it is *possible* to be both Western and

Turkish–Muslim. Most people in Edremit seem to feel that, for their own part, it is perfectly possible. The anxiety centers upon whether Turkey's commitment to the West will be reciprocated, most especially, of course, with respect to relations with Greece, for example, in connection with the Cyprus question. The suspicion, characteristic of both secularist and committed Muslim, that, despite Turkey's enthusiastic membership in NATO, the West's instinctive Christianity and philhellenism will lead it "always to support the country where there are many people named George," as I heard one Edremit man put it, is a strong reinforcement to the Islamic side of Turkish identity.

But the cultural compromise is also a synthesis. An excellent illustration of this process is provided by the recent revival of Islamic education in the form of Schools for Imams and Preachers. These were first opened during the political relaxation of the 1940s to train religious professionals, the supply of which had been depleted during the years of rigorous secularism. Increasingly, however, these schools are seen as an alternative to the regular middle schools and secondary schools (*lises*) for parents who would like their children to receive more than the token religious instruction offered by the secular institutions. Consequently, they are springing up all over the country. These schools, and the Higher Islamic Institutes into which they feed, teach a secular curriculum as well as religious knowledge and their graduates are now claiming entrance to the universities on the same footing as graduates of the secular schools.

In Edremit, as in other towns, a School for Imams and Preachers is being created by the same process that brought into being many of the town's other amenities, that is, unofficial philanthropy. Giving for the public good is strongly supported by Islamic tradition and by the local common culture.

Municipalities in Turkey are held on short rein by the central government; they may not, for example, raise special taxes or rates. But, building on gifts from the town's rich men, merchants collect a kind of voluntary tax on retail transactions. A building is built, and the government is then persuaded to provide staff. Edremit's secondary school (*lise*) and the tuberculosis wing of its hospital were created by this means.

The Imams and Preachers school has its opponents, and not only among the "enlightened," for there are secularists among the local merchants and craftsmen, as well as among teachers and civil servants. Ideology and occupation (or "class") seldom correlate perfectly anywhere in the world — a circumstance which contributes greatly to civility, however much it may discomfit social scientists. But the strongest supporters, apart from the *hocas,* are indeed the small merchants and artisans. For them the school represents not only a fuller Islamic education but also a broadening of opportunity for upward mobility, since the children of the "enlightened" have tended to dominate both the secular schools and the elite into which they lead. To perhaps a majority in Edremit, including many who prefer the secular schools for their own children, the new school represents both a filling-out of the complement of amenities necessary to a civilized (*medeni*) town and a broadening of personal choice.

This last point is crucial. Repeatedly in our conversations with townspeople about religion and reform we heard such phrases as *"şimdi huzur içindeyiz," "daha hürriyet var şimdi," "taasub, musamahasızlık azaldı"*: "now we're at ease," "there's more freedom now," "bigotry and intolerance have declined." Whether the subject is education or women's dress and demeanor or the practice of religion, people will express their own views and then add, "Of course, we are free to choose."

Excessively puritanical *hocas* are criticized for "always forbidding everything," just as are any officials or teachers who might offend local standards of propriety or flaunt irreligion. People clearly value increased tolerance and openness, as a definite improvement over both the religious rigor which, they say, constricted progress in the time of their ancestors, and the severe reformism of the one–party period of the Republic. Ottoman gendarmes, they say (perhaps stretching the literal truth), arrested women who dropped the veil, while early Republican ones abused women who refused to abandon it. This broadening of choice is the provincial counterpart of the striking freedom of expression which today (1970) fills the bookstores and newsstands of the cities with examples of every conceivable shade of opinion.

The compromise, or synthesis, which emerges from the experience and experiment of everyday life in the microcosms of the provincial city is not, therefore, merely a different mixture of sociocultural elements. It is also a more open, more relaxed milieu in which freedom of choice has taken its place as a positively–valued cultural strand and a reality of social experience. In this sense, liberal democracy has taken root in Edremit.

But this has not taken place in isolation from events in the central arenas of the larger society, as I hope I have made clear. It lies beyond the scope of this discussion to trace the interaction of national and local events through the single–party and multi–party periods, but perhaps a single recent example will serve to illustrate.

In the spring of 1969, politics — always a favorite topic of conversation — were more than usually in the air because general elections were to be held in October. In May a series of disturbing and violent events filled the newspapers: clashes among students and between students and police had for more than a year prevented the major universities from functioning normally; the small parties of the extreme right and left issued threatening statements; the leaders of the banned Democrat Party who had been deprived of their political rights were demanding their reinstatement and were supported in their demand by the right wing of Prime Minister Demirel's ruling Justice Party.

Against this background, a secularist judge of the Supreme Court, who had made his agnostic views known, died. In the course of his funeral at a mosque in Ankara, religious conservatives attempted to disrupt the proceedings on the ground that the deceased had been an atheist (*dinsiz*) and clashed with secularist students. Ex-Prime Minister İnönü, himself strongly identified with secularism, was present, and allegedly in order to protect him from possible attack by the demonstrators, an army general drew his pistol. The services were transferred to another mosque. Next day the papers were filled with demands by secularists for "firm measures against religious reaction." In support of these demands, secularists, led by high court judges, paraded down Atatürk Boulevard in Ankara and it was suggested that the national organization of religious professionals has been behind the disruption of the funeral. There were ominous front page accounts of a two-and-one-half-hour conference between the Prime Minister and the President, an ex-general.

During the weeks following, while the Prime Minister was beset by demands for "firm measures," the elderly but vigorous İnönü took the political initiative. In a surprise move designed to discredit the Prime Minister with his own right wing, he staged a well-publicized reconciliation with Celal Bayar, who had been president during the Democrat administration, and came out for restoration of rights to the Democrat leaders. He also let it be known that he had opposed the execution of the

three Democrats in 1961 and declared that military intervention now would be unjustified. By the end of May, while the
students were still clashing, tension subsided somewhat.
Constitution Day, May 27, which commemorates the 1960
military coup, passed without the rumored intervention by the
army.

In Edremit, people were stirred by these events and they were
widely discussed. The teachers and officials whose views we
heard felt strongly that the government should "crack down on
religious reaction." So also did one of the town's leading
business men, an immigrant from eastern Europe with advanced social views. A young olive grower, president of the
local "Nationalist Society," became more vocal in his denunciations of "communists in the universities." A tailor was
worried about military intervention and strongly opposed it.
"It should not be," he said, "because the people are against it."
The intervention of 1960, he thought, had been justified. He
generally supports the Republican Peoples' Party and he
agreed with a newspaper which described İnönü's initiatives as
the work of a true political craftsman — a "fox's fox." A retired
military officer said that there would be no intervention. His
son, a serving officer, had heard rumors of an alert, but these,
he said, were spread by communists and Masons. We heard no
one openly advocate military intervention.

On May 27, Constitution Day, the local army training unit
staged its usual parade up the main street and around the
square. The commanding general took the salute from a
reviewing stand, along with the mayor, the county governor
and other dignitaries. Then, standing in a jeep, he drove slowly
around the square shouting greetings to the sparse crowd. Only
school children, who had been coached, shouted back the expected reply. After the laying of wreaths at the Atatürk statue,
as the crowd drifted away, a friend with whom we had been

watching — a political middle-of-the-roader — remarked
that those who most disapproved of military intervention had
simply stayed at home.

The next day was the Birthday of the Prophet and in the
evening the mosques were filled. Among those present, his
young son at his side, was a teacher who had been most insistent upon strong action against the "religious bigots" who
had disrupted the judge's funeral.

The following five months brought more turmoil in the
universities, mutual denunciations among the parties and a rising crescenco of noise and posturing by the extreme right and
left which, if one were to judge from the newspapers, seemed to
be polarizing Turkish politics. Then, in October, Edremit and
the nation went to the polls. The national result was a slight
gain for the Republican Peoples' Party, a moderate loss for the
Justice Party, although the Prime Minister retained a
parliamentary majority, and losses for the parties of the extreme left and right (see Appendix D to this chapter). The voting in Edremit followed a similar pattern. For now, at any rate,
most Turks, here as elsewhere, had responded to crisis at the
center of their society by opting for tranquility and tolerance.

* * * * *

My account of the Turkish venture in nation-statehood
must break off with the summer of 1970, when I last visited
Edremit. I make no attempt to recount the turbulent events of
the past two years except to recall that the confrontations
between small groups of religious conservatives and extreme
secularists in the metropolitan centers continued; turmoil in
the universities increased and many were temporarily closed
down; a small but disciplined body of leftist guerrillas emerged
and engaged in acts of terrorism; and in March, 1971, the
military did, finally, intervene. They did not seize power, as in

1960, but instead established martial law in several provinces and forced a change of government "in order to suppress terrorism and carry out further reform." There were many arrests and trials before special courts and freedom of the press was curtailed. Parliament, however, stubbornly remained in session, the two major parties demonstrating a striking solidarity in the face of military pressure. More recently, elections have been announced for October, 1973.

There, for the moment, I must leave a story which I hope to continue to follow, with only the observation that, if the past is any guide to the future, Turks will continue their project of constructing a national reality as both Muslims and secular republicans. On the one hand, any return to an "Islamic state" — to a caliphate or to a state-enforced Islamic law — seems quite out of the question, because a half-century of republican life (not to speak of the century or more of preparation for it) has left the vast majority of Turks not only opposed to such a return but also with only the vaguest conception of what it might involve. On the other hand, those same years have shown how firmly an equally large majority remain attached to the House of Islam. They remain attached in various senses, for the "Islamic revival" of the post-Second World War period is far from monolithic; rather, it is a many-stranded seeking for the meaning of an ancient faith in the new republican setting. With the greatest hesitation I hazard a guess at what may lie beyond the tentative synthesis I described earlier, that is, beyond the growing attachment to openness and choice in public life.

Beyond this there are, I think, possibilities for a convergence of religious and republican sentiments upon greater stress on social justice. The Kemalist state, despite its populist rhetoric, placed greater emphasis upon secularization than upon popular participation, gave greater attention to increasing national wealth than to its just distribution. These were no doubt the most urgent tasks at the time, but Turkey is no longer the ragged and untutored country inherited by Atatürk from the Ottomans. Still backward and poor by Western European standards, the country is advanced and rich by the standards of the Third World. Within recent years there has been a perceptible shift toward a "left-of-center," social democratic position within the Republican People's Party (Ecevit 1966) and toward a more welfare state capitalist position on the part of the Justice Party.[13]

If such shifts were to continue, they would converge with that important strand in Turkish Islam which asserts the brotherhood of all Muslims — a strand that may easily be detected in the conversation of people in Edremit. Rich men who do not give generously to philanthropic projects are severely criticized on religious grounds. Handbooks of Islamic teaching on business ethics are read. I once heard one man upbraid another in the public street for mistreating his apprentices and not paying them sufficiently well. The work place is viewed as analogous to a school in its influence upon the character of the young apprentice and therefore its moral climate is a legitimate subject for public concern. Enterprise (çalışkanlık) is much admired, but the successful man who, for example, invests in real estate to make an easy, speculative profit is not; he ought to invest in industry "for the good of the country." These are not "radical" views, but rather those of pious, rather conservative men.

13. Justice Party governments have moved toward greater provision of social services such as schools and hospitals.

## Postscript, 1974

The elections of October, 1973, which were held on schedule, may mark a watershed in recent Turkish politics. For the first time since the beginning of multi-party competition, the Republican Peoples' Party, now under "left of center" leadership, received a plurality of the vote (see Appendix D to this chapter). Furthermore, a new religiously-oriented party, the National Salvation Party, representing the Islamic populism and egalitarianism of Turkey's small businessmen and craftsmen, received 12 percent of the vote. The R.P.P. and the N.S.P. went into coalition to form the new government under the premiership of Bulent Ecevit, the "left of center" leader. What had seemed the eternal verities of Turkish politics had shifted sufficiently so that the party of Atatürk, historically the party of secularist reform, could work with a religiously-oriented party on the basis of a similar outlook on economic affairs — or, at any rate, a common opposition to domination of the economy by "big business."

Whether the coalition will prove to be a durable one remains to be seen. Its formation required three months of difficult negotiations. If it does survive, the *kulturkampf* between religion and secularism may well recede from the prominent place it has held in Turkish politics and economic questions may become more salient.

However, I must now turn to what appear to me to be the hazards of such speculations about the future.

## APPENDIX A
## CHRONICLE OF EVENTS IN EDREMIT*

1443 B.C.:          City founded by Lydians of the empire of Croesus.

548 B.C.:           Captured by Alexander the Great, annexed to Greek Ionia.

129 B.C.:           Captured by the Romans.

1076-1206 A.D.:     City passes from Byzantium to the Seljuk Turks to Byzantium to Frederick Barbarossa's crusaders to the Latin Empire of Constantinople and back to Byzantium.

1231 A.D.:          Captured by Seljuk captain Yusuf Sinan.

1341 A.D.:          The City and its region annexed to the Ottoman Turkish Empire.

(Five hundred years of earthquakes, fires, revolts by the Greek population, successions of beys and pashas, visits by sultans, building of mosques.)

1877:               Arrival of refugees from former Ottoman Lands in Europe.

1880:               First dues–paying social club founded.

1883:               First powered sawmill.

1885:               Gas–works built; first modern olive oil press with filtration system.

1888:               First modern primary school.

1889:               Chamber of Commerce founded.

1890:               First pharmacy.

1897:               A reserve battalion goes to the Greek War; the city now has three physicians.

1899:               A refugee party of 24 houses arrives from Crete.

1906:               Ceremony of thanksgiving for escape of Sultan Abdül Hamid from assassination.

1909: Arrival of the first traveling cinema; the Union and Progress Party sends material to the army.

1910: First electric light.

1912: Of the Edremit battalion sent to the Balkan War, four remain alive; refugees from the Balkans and the Aegean islands arrive.

1913: First automobile; Edremit buys an airplane for the Turkish forces; the airplane flies to Cairo.

1914: World War I; revolt by Greek population put down; Jihad ("holy war") is declared; a military hospital is built.

1915: Bombardment by English fleet; guns of the Gallipoli campaign heard in the city; German commander Liman von Sanders passes through; clothing sent to the troops; third draft of men for World War I.

1917: Of the reserve officers called up in June only three remain alive; all others have "fallen as martyrs"; Mevlûd ceremony for the dead.

1919: Governor Hamdi Bey founds a school and athletic society; a Defense of Rights Society is founded; Gov. Hamdi Bey dismissed by government in İstanbul, now under the control of Allied occupation; money being collected in the villages for nationalist forces (resistance); İzmir is occupied by the Greeks; Mustafa Kemal telegraphs encouragement to local Defense of Rights Society; nationalist irregulars operating in the mountains.

1920: Governor Hamdi Bey dies a martyr with nationalist irregulars; Greeks occupy the city; deportations of notables and intellectuals.

1921: Battles between Greeks and nationalist irregulars; sabotage against Greeks and fierce retaliation.

1922: Greeks driven out after 797 days of occupation; collaborators lynched.

1923:           Visit by National Commander Gazi Mustafa Kemal Pasha.

1924:           Republican Peoples' Party branch founded.

1925:           First hats worn under new "Hat Law"; *Edremit* newspaper founded.

1926:           Marriage office opened under new civil law; first radio.

1927:           Beating of drums to announce Ramadan forbidden.

1929:           Dance pavilion built; adult night school founded to teach latin orthography.

1932:           Agricultural credit cooperative founded.

1935:           "Peoples' House" (political–cultural center) opened.

1938:           Death of "our great father, Atatürk"; general mourning.

1941:           Visit by President İsmet İnönü.

1946:           Democrat Party branch founded.

1950:           Free elections; Democrat Party comes to power.

*Selected from Yetkin (1957). For the Byzantine and early Turkish period see Vryonis (1971).

## APPENDIX B

# THE OCCUPATIONAL STRUCTURE OF EDREMIT, 1965*
(women in brackets)

*Technicians, Free Professions and Related*

| | |
|---|---|
| Architects, engineers and related | 11 |
| Technicians and scientific officials | 18 |
| Agricultural and forestry technicians | 8 |
| Pharmacists and apprentices | 9 ( 1) |
| Medical and related | 74 ( 25) |
| Teachers | 178 ( 37) |
| Law (judges, advocates, prosecutors) | 19 |
| Artists (writers, painters, musicians, entertainers) | 64 ( 13) |
| Imams and preachers | 35 |
| Others (all accountants) | 7 |
| Total | 423 ( 76): 8% |

*Entrepreneurs, Managers, Office Workers*

| | |
|---|---|
| Officials in state service | 21 |
| Wholesale and retail managers and entrepreneurs | 50 |
| Financial (banks and insurance) | 9 |
| Real Estate | 4 |
| Extraction, manufacturing, building | 46 ( 2) |
| Other entrepreneurs and managers | 41 |
| Bookkeepers, cashiers, secretaries | 250 ( 22) |
| Total | 421 ( 24): 8% |

*Commercial workers ("sellers")*

| | |
|---|---|
| Retail and wholesale merchants and employees | 395 ( 4) |
| Itinerant merchants and peddlers | 193 ( 2) |
| Others | 18 |
| Total | 606 ( 6): 11% |

*Farmers, lumbermen, fishermen*

| | | |
|---|---:|---|
| Farmers, farm managers | 391 | ( 10) |
| Truck gardeners | 214 | ( 29) |
| Orchard and vinyard farmers | 36 | ( 4) |
| Farm and forest machine operators | 4 | |
| Herdsmen and shepherds | 43 | |
| Fishermen | 21 | |
| Farm laborers | 328 | ( 25) |
| Total | 1037 | ( 68): 19% |

*Mining, quarrying*

| | | |
|---|---:|---|
| Total | 17 | ( 0): .3% |

*Transport & communications*

| | | |
|---|---:|---|
| Sea transport | 7 | |
| Motor drivers | 186 | ( 1) |
| Animal transport | 140 | |
| Postal workers | 28 | ( 5) |
| Others | 39 | |
| Total | 400 | ( 6): 7% |

*Craftsmen and repairers*

| | | |
|---|---:|---|
| Casting and forging | 8 | |
| Metal manufacturing and repair | 308 | |
| Electric goods manufacturing and repair | 32 | |
| Textile weavers | 30 | ( 4) |
| Tailors, shoemakers, quilt and mattress makers | 387 | ( 67) |
| Wood and cane workers | 168 | ( 1) |
| Food, drink, tobacco manufacture | 157 | ( 1) |
| Construction workers | 205 | |
| Stone and clay fabricators | 27 | |
| Other | 77 | ( 2) |
| Total | 1399 | ( 75): 25% |

*Unskilled workers*

| | | |
|---|---:|---|
| Total | 459 | ( 2): 8% |

*Services*
| | |
|---|---|
| Servants, waiters, cooks | 356 ( 47) |
| Barbers, bath attendants, coiffeurs, dry cleaners, launderers | 200 ( 18) |
| Security services | 164 ( 2) |
| Total | 720 ( 67): 13% |

*Not assigned to occupations*
| | |
|---|---|
| Military | 6802 ( 1) |
| Other | 65 ( 1) |
| Total | 6867 ( 2): 56% |
| | |
| Total | 12355 (326) |
| Less military** | 5488 (325): 99% |

*Data generously provided from the 1965 census by the State Institute of Statistics.
**Above percentages based upon this total.

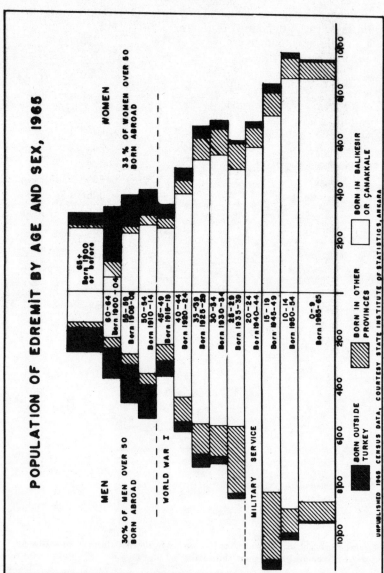

## APPENDIX C

POPULATION OF EDREMİT BY AGE AND SEX, 1965

MEN

30% OF MEN OVER 50 BORN ABROAD

WORLD WAR I

MILITARY SERVICE

WOMEN

33 % OF WOMEN OVER 50 BORN ABROAD

65+
Born 1900
or before

60-64
Born 1900-04

55-59
Born 1905-09

50-54
Born 1910-14

45-49
Born 1910-19

40-44
Born 1920-24

35-39
Born 1925-29

30-34
Born 1930-34

25-29
Born 1935-39

20-24
Born 1940-44

15-19
Born 1945-49

10-14
Born 1950-54

0-9
Born 1955-65

10|00    8|00    6|00    4|00    2|00    2|00    4|00    6|00    8|00    10|00

BORN OUTSIDE TURKEY

BORN IN OTHER PROVINCES

BORN IN BALIKESIR OR ÇANAKKALE

UNPUBLISHED 1965 CENSUS DATA, COURTESY STATE INSTITUTE OF STATISTICS, ANKARA

# APPENDIX D

## ELECTIONS OF 1965, 1969 AND 1973:
## PERCENT OF THE VOTE

| | Edremit City | | | Province | | | Turkey | | |
|---|---|---|---|---|---|---|---|---|---|
| | 1965 | 1969 | 1973 | 1965 | 1969 | 1973 | 1965 | 1969 | 1973 |
| Justice Party | 64 | 60 | ? | 63 | 56 | ? | 53 | 47 | 30 |
| Republican People's Party | 29 | 31 | | 29 | 29 | | 29 | 27 | 33 |
| Reliance Party* | — | 2 | | — | 5 | | — | 7 | 5 |
| Nation Party | 2 | 3 | | 3 | 1 | | 6 | 3 | — |
| National Action Party** | 1 | 1 | | 1 | 2 | | 2 | 3 | 4 |
| Unity Party*** | — | 1 | | — | 2 | | — | 3 | 1 |
| Turkish Workers' Party | 3 | 2 | | 2 | 3 | | 3 | 3 | — |
| New Turkey Party | 1 | 1 | | 1 | 1 | | 4 | 2 | — |
| National Salvation Party**** | — | — | | — | — | | — | — | 12 |
| Independents | 1- | 1- | | 1- | 1- | | 3 | 6 | 3 |
| Democratic Party**** | — | — | | — | — | | — | — | 12 |

*Split off from R.P.P. between 1965 and 1969 elections.
**In 1965 called Republican Peasants' Nation Party.
***Formed between 1965 and 1969 elections; appeals especially to Alevis.
****Formed between 1969 and 1973 elections.

Note: The National Action Party forms the extreme "right" (fascist), the Turkish Workers' Party, banned in 1973, the extreme "left" (Marxist).

Sources: *1950-1969 Milletvekili ve 1961, 1964 Senatosu Uye Seçimleri Sonucları.* Ankara: State Institute of Statistics, 1966; *Cumhuriyet* newspaper; *Edremit* newspaper.

# four

# THE PROBLEM
# OF THE FUTURE

Our manifest destiny is to overspread the continent allotted by Providence for the free development of our yearly multiplying millions.

JOHN LOUIS O'SULLIVAN, 1845

The theory that God reveals Himself and His
judgement in history is indistinguishable from the
theory that worldly success is the ultimate judge
and justification of our actions; it comes to the
same thing as the doctrine that history will judge,
that is to say, that future might is right . . . . To
maintain that God reveals Himself in what is
usually called "history," in the history of international crime and of mass murder, is indeed
blasphemy . . . .

KARL POPPER, 1946

In the last chapter, I shall return to the concerns which I
outlined in a preliminary way in the first: that is, the role of the
social anthropological style of inquiry in the study of the
contemporary nation–state. Thus far I have made some initial
suggestions concerning the relationship of that sort of inquiry,
which I termed "microcosmic," and other, more "macrocosmic," views of the nation–state. I have tried to apply these
notions, again in a rather broad and preliminary manner, to
the experience of East Africa and to that of Turkey. I want to
review these ideas and data in relation to some prevailing
modes of thought and research. But first it is necessary to con-
front a problem which to this point I have mentioned in only

117

the most oblique way, but toward which an attitude must be adopted if one is to think clearly about the contemporary nation–state: that is, the problem of the future.

In the last chapter and its predecessor, I took leave of the Turks and the East Africans with some rather ambiguous remarks concerning their possible respective futures. The ambiguity was deliberate, but it was left unexplained. I felt that I — or indeed any observer of East African or Turkish affairs — could not reasonably go beyond a statement of certain sociocultural parameters and tendencies, but I did not attempt to justify this view.

This reluctance to predict or, more accurately, to prophesy, requires amplification because many social scientists regard knowledge about the future of societies or nations as a major goal and justification of their work. Furthermore, contemporary nation–states themselves are expected by their people and their leaders to be future–oriented. And this is the case not only in the new states of the Third World. In the West, too, and perhaps especially in the United States, social criticism emphasizes the need for "fundamental social change" — often, to be sure, with little specification of what is to be changed, and how, and toward what end. "Futurology" has made its appearance as an alleged field of study and scholars and scientists have organized a "Committee on the year 2000." Sociologists and anthropologists scrutinize each others' work for signs that its presuppositions are "static," and hence bad, or "able to account for change," and therefore good. Plainly there is in much of this acclaim of "change" a good deal less, intellectually, than meets the eye; there is also in it a good deal of ambiguity as to whether the main problem for societies is creating change or coping with its consequences.

Nevertheless it is clear that change and the expectation of change are fundamental to the condition of contemporary societies, east, west and south, and if this is true of societies as macrocosms, there must follow consequences for the microcosms within which their people live. How, then, may we most usefully conceptualize sociocultural change and the impulse toward change, both macrocosmic and microcosmic?

A careful consideration of this problem is made particularly urgent, in my view, by a recent widespread retreat in the social sciences toward certainty about the future — toward a revival of evolutionary theorizing, that is to say, theorizing designed to discern the inevitable direction of human history. The problem is important because if it *is* possible to know in advance the course history will inevitably take, then the central element in the view of human affairs adopted in these lectures, namely, the intentional actor, drops out, is obliterated, and becomes meaningless. Perhaps the most interesting — and ironical — example of the evolutionary revival is that of Talcott Parsons, whose most important work, *The Structure of Social Action* (1937), opened with the words, "Who now reads Spencer?" The answer, to most readers in the 1930s, was plain: Herbert Spencer stood for all the many nineteenth century theorists of sociocultural evolution, and the ideas of all of them were equally presumed to be dead. Such theorizing, Parsons felt in 1937, was sterile because it, like other positivistic theories, robbed human social action of its "voluntaristic" element — the element of meaning-creation and that of choice, notions which become meaningless in any theory of historical inevitability. Now, however, as a result of what Parsons sees as "major theoretical and empirical advances that have accumulated since the earlier evolutionists wrote," he believes that the idea has become "enormously more fruitful," indeed "essential" (1966:109). And Parsons is not, of course, alone. Lewis Henry Morgan's evolutionary ideas have been revived and extended by Leslie White and his students (White 1959;

Sahlins and Service 1960), and many other social scientists have joined them.

The idea of evolution tends, intrinsically, to be infused with evaluation. One must decide, if one makes use of it, in what direction historical inevitability is leading and, although it is logically possible to be depressed by this prevision, the leading proponents of the idea have always tended to side with the inexorable. But sociocultural prophecy today, as in the past, attracts persons with a diversity of prophetic visions. Between Herbert Spencer and Karl Marx, between Leslie White and Talcott Parsons (and their respective epigoni), differences of view concerning the direction in which we are tending are broad enough to accommodate every taste. When the evolutionists argue about whether Mao's China or some kind of purified version of twentieth century North America represents the wave of the future, it is possible to discuss the ideas they share with a good deal of detachment.

This revival of evolutionary theorizing — in the sense of theorizing designed to discern the inevitable direction of history, whether on the level of the whole human community or on that of its constituent communities — is clearly a movement of some consequence in contemporary social science. Even discounting the faddish use of the term, which today, as in the nineteenth century, has given it a surface currency not always underpinned by serious evolutionary thinking, the volume of prophetic writing swells from year to year and it encounters remarkably little resistance in the form of critical review. There are, of course, dissenting views. As the distinguished English biologist P.B. Medawar has remarked in his Spencer lecture of 1963, "[Spencer's] is a philosophy for the age of steam; and until a few years ago we should have been tempted to describe it as equally out of date in content. Evidently it is not . . . in recent years his ideas have come back to life, or been propped upright again . . . ." (Medawar 1963:35).

In what follows I shall review some of the commoner arguments about the idea of sociocultural evolution and ask whether, indeed, "major theoretical and empirical advances" have made the contemporary brand more useful than the product marketed by Marx and Spencer in the nineteenth century.

First, let us turn to the semantic problem. While the word "evolution" has a long and varied history, the area of science in which it has achieved a consensual meaning as a frame of reference for a vigorous and continuing body of research is, of course, biology. In that field today it means processes of biological change in populations, involving genetic variation and adaptation through selective mating. It does not, for most biologists today, mean an overall, continuous, directional change in the biological world as a whole, and its larger course is "inevitable" only in the sense that the contemporary situation is the result of ". . . historical causation, which includes everything that has ever happened and which is thus an inherently nonrepeatable accumulation." The *processes* of biological evolution are general and predictable, *given specific conditions;* the *actual biological course of events* (biological history) is particular and not subject to generalization, much less to prophecy (Roe and Simpson 1958:21-26).

Neglect of the difference between prediction under specifiable conditions and prophecy about the concrete future has been one root of the misunderstanding between biological and sociocultural "evolutionists," for it is precisely generalization concerning the concrete course of history that sociocultural evolutionism is all about. Citing the work of Sahlins and Service, Dobzhansky writes:

A biologist cannot fail to note that "general evolution" sounds very much like what on the biological level is represented by the hypothesis of autogenesis or orthogenesis . . . . This notion proved to be unprofitable as a working hypothesis and is now a minority view. (1962:10)

Of course it is common for words to be used in rather different senses in different fields of inquiry and there is no reason why this should not be so, provided we are clear about what we are doing. The term "structure," for example, has some residue of common meaning across the fields of social anthropology, literary criticism and crystallography. The more particular meanings it assumes in relation to other terms in each of these spheres of discourse do not usually get in each other's way because they normally are neither applied to the same data nor transferred from one field to the other analogically. But both sources of confusion commonly occur between the biological and sociocultural uses of "evolution," perhaps because both biological and sociocultural processes of change have played critical, and interacting, roles in the actual human career, and also because the successes of evolutionary biology have created an intellectual climate receptive to the analogical use of its concepts in sociocultural studies.

Everyone agrees, of course, that the processes of "evolution" are different in the two fields. Intergenerational transmission involves different kinds of processes — biochemical in the one case, socio- cultural-psychological in the other — and is much more "determinate" in biology than in the sociocultural realm, where selection and adaptation are more Lamarckian than Darwinian. Medawar argues,

Common sense suggests that differences of this magnitude should be acknowledged by a distinction of terminology. The use of the word "evolution" for psychological change is not a natural usage, but an artificial usage adopted by theorists with an axe to grind. (1963:39)

"Natural" is perhaps not the best word, given the frequency and antiquity of the usage in question; indeed Robert Nisbet

(1969) has recently written at length, and rather persuasively, about its recurrent popularity in the Western intellectual tradition. Nevertheless, it is quite clear that the analogy with biology suggested today by the terms "cultural evolution" or "social evolution" is less than complete.

What the two usages have most in common is the concept of "adaptation." But before considering the significance of adaptive processes in biological and sociocultural change, it is necessary to return for a bit to the Big Picture — to the problem of generalization about the overall direction of change and of prophecy concerning its future course. We have seen that biologists, on the whole, find the notion of "general evolution" unhelpful. There are directional trends in biological change, but these never continue indefinitely; within the biological world — the biosphere — as a whole, biologists find no discernible continuous trend. It is therefore difficult to see from whom, among biologists, Parsons — who is concerned to stress the continuity of his thought with theirs — has come by his conviction that "to be an evolutionist, one must define a general trend in evolution . . . ." (1966:109).

White and his followers rest their general evolutionary theorizing upon the second law of thermodynamics and the antithermodynamic properties of living matter: in the cosmos as a whole, matter is breaking down and energy is becoming more uniformly diffused, but organisms draw upon the energy thus freed to build up increasingly complex biological systems. Sociocultural systems simply extend this process. Whatever may be said for this scheme as cosmology, it seems to have little to do with the actual work of evolutionary biologists. "In my opinion," Medawar concludes, "the audacious attempt to reveal the formal equivalence of the ideas of biological organization and of thermodynamic order, non–randomness, and information must be judged to have failed." (1963:43).

But even if the theorists of "general evolution" find little support in contemporary biology, it is of course possible that the idea has a merit when applied to society and culture that it lacks in the biological sciences. Setting aside the problem of continuities and analogies with organic evolution, is it not possible — indeed rather easy — to discern grand trends in sociocultural history? Of course it is. On any of a series of criteria — social organizational and cultural complexity, material productivity, control of energy, storage of information, and so forth — one may easily demonstrate a rise, even an exponential rise, from whatever point in the Pleistocene one wishes to choose to mark the emergence of biologically modern man until the present day. True, striking such a line may involve a good deal of evening-off: there have been periods of stagnation and even reversals. But the trend is clear: some countries, and perhaps even the human community as a whole (with differences evened out), have become enormously more complex, more productive and better-informed than their predecessors. But all this is obvious to the point of banality, and useless, too, since, as with the idea of "general evolution" or orthogenesis in biology, it provides no basis for empirical inquiry. If we accept the evolutionary trend as a hypothesis rather than an article of faith (in the latter case, of course, the question of inquiry does not arise), it is possible, in principle, to predict its continuation, but to render such a prediction testable it is necessary to specify conditions, including temporal duration. The statement that "*in the long run,* the trend will hold" is inherently unfalsifiable.

Karl Popper, in a powerful critique of the idea of historical inevitability which has received remarkably little attention by the theorists of evolution, arrives at the same conclusion:

> The decisive step in this argument is . . . *if there is such a thing as growing human knowledge, then we cannot anticipate today what*

*we shall know only tomorrow . . . . No scientific predictor —*
whether a human scientist or a calculating machine — can possibly
predict, by scientific methods, its own future results. Attempts to
do so can attain their result only after the event, when it is too late
for a prediction; they can attain their result only after the prediction has turned into retrodiction . . . this means that no society
can predict, scientifically, its own future states of knowledge.
(1957:x)

Nor, it follows, can it predict its own future choices.

But what Parsons, White and the others are engaged in is
precisely retrodiction — a selective recitation of history
designed to lend an aura of directionality and inevitability to
man's advance from a hunting–and–gathering life to that
characteristic of present–day United States, with a bit of
prophecy thrown in at the end. Parsons himself, as seems to be
conventional in the genre, begins with the Australian
aborigines. (Why not the Bushmen? What warrant indeed, as
archeologists are beginning to ask themselves, for assuming
that *any* of the historically known hunting–and–gathering
peoples closely approximate our Pleistocene ancestors in their
sociocultural life?) He then guides us along through "advanced
primitive" societies to Egypt, Mesopotamia, the New World
civilizations, classical antiquity and the oriental empires. The
story is not uninteresting, for Parsons adds much sociological
insight to conventional history, principally through his
analyses in terms of sociocultural differentiation. His
treatment of Israel and Greece as "seed–bed" societies
(1966:95-106) — societies whose societal autonomy was
snuffed out by more powerful neighbors, but whose cultures
survived to deeply influence later developments in the West —
is hardly original, but it is interesting and it demonstrates that
he is too learned a man to be taken in entirely by the
food–and–hardware, up–from–the–ape school of evolution.
Indeed, as he proceeds on to "modernity," the account reads

more and more like sociocultural history and less and less like
evolution. Nevertheless, the history has a plot: all that has gone
before leads inexorably to the United States as the "lead
society" in "generalized adaptive capacity" (Parsons 1971:3,
86-121).

In one sense this is unexceptionable. The United States is in
many ways the most differentiated and powerful of contemporary national societies, and there is, of course, a sense in
which it is the product of an extended network of events leading backward into prehistory. Given all those events, contemporary America was "inevitable." The critical question,
however, is whether or not, *from the vantage point of any
society or period or "stage" in the past, all that followed, including present-day U.S. society, was inevitable;* that is the
standpoint we adopt when we attempt to forecast our own
future. Was it inevitable in Pericles' time, and from his van-
tage-point, (even granting Pericles Parsons' understanding of
evolution), that, — to choose an example which Parsons con-
siders important to his "evolutionary" account — crucial
developments in the field of law and government should take
place a few centuries later in nearby Italy? Could it actually
have been forseen with some confidence in the age of Henry
VIII that North America would become the most fertile
ground for capitalism and protestantism? Did not the insights
and judgments of particular men and groups of men — located,
of course, in particular ecological, historical and sociocultural
contexts — play some substantial role in these developments,
and were these insights and judgments, even given their contexts, really inevitable? Might they not, quite easily, have been
different — different enough to matter? The evening off involved in striking the evolutionary "trend" obscures these
questions. While mankind has thus far managed to soldier
along in the *general* direction of greater power, wealth and

sophistication, the geographic centers of maximal development of these qualities have varied greatly from millennium to millennium and even from century to century. And the more closely one examines a particular place and period the more difficult it becomes to discern what the "next stage" will be — provided, of course, one is able to perform the intellectual contortion of excluding from consideration all knowledge of what in fact did happen later. That latter condition, however, is extremely difficult; uncontaminated prediction is possible only from the vantage point of one's own present.

Perhaps, though, Parsons does not mean to claim prophetic powers for his evolutionary scheme. Certainly he becomes vague enough when he comes to his discussion of the future.

> It is our conviction that, though major changes are in process, the sociologist of the twenty–first century will discern just as many factors of continuity with the past as we can now discern with the nineteenth century and, of course, those previous to it. This *conviction*, however, is not a *prediction*, which the critic could legitimately insist be stated more precisely or retracted . . . . It is our *conviction* that the coming phase will center on integrating the consequences of (the industrial, democratic and educational) revolutions, both mutually and with the societal community. (Parsons 1971:143)

A similar vagueness pervades the prophecies of Peacock and Kirsch. In the final chapters of their recent evolutionary textbook, they provide a melange of extrapolations drawn largely from contemporary American pop and youth culture, "death of God" theology, Marcusian ideas of alienation, Macluhanism and political–economic romanticism. They succeed only in demonstrating the force of Popper's critique:

> If a trend (they write) can be anticipated to continue, it is reasonably safe to extrapolate from that trend and predict "the present, but more of it." But if the next level of sociocultural evolution is to be drastically different from the present one —

different not merely in degree but in kind — simply predicting more of the present would be grossly misleading. (Peacock and Kirsch 1970:288)

Therefore, they say, one must go back to the "mechanism" which past sociocultural evolution (development in determinate directions through persistent processes of change) shows to have operated in the emergence of new levels. This mechanism is dissonance among social, cultural and psychological systems and the tendency of culture to "render meaningful an advance in social modernity and complexity [by] 'transcendentaliz[ing]' the old cultural pattern from which it derives" (Peacock and Kirsch 1970:293). As transcendent gods or "cosmic orders" replaced god–kings, so the search for a transcendent beyond god (who has died) will drive positivist modern man to seek transcendence within the self.

God may or may not have died, but in this formulation of transcendentalization as a "mechanism" of evolution, the voluntaristic theory of action, on which these writers, as students of Parsons, may be presumed to have cut their intellectual teeth, has certainly done so. With all due respect (for these are people who have done excellent work), the next "level of sociocultural evolution" bears a suspicious resemblance to the narcissistic preoccupations of many present–day academic intellectuals — or perhaps to those of intellectuals in most times and places. When prophecy through extrapolation fails, where else is there to seek for the future but within the self?

Robert Bellah, another of Parsons' students, has applied the evolutionary idiom to the unlikely subject of religion. Bellah is certainly a very learned scholar who has contributed much to the study of that subject, not only through his well–known monograph on Tokugawa Japan (1957) but also through a series of thoughtful papers recently republished in a volume entitled *Beyond Belief,* which includes the paper on "Religious Evolution" (1970:20-45). His knowledge of religions, past and present, is enviable and he handles his materials with a sensitivity born of a personal involvement with man's enduring dilemmas. Nevertheless, in the paper in question his treatment illustrates a feature common in evolutionary writing, namely the desire to have it both ways — to concede the flaws in evolutionary thinking and yet to preserve its basic assumptions. He opens his argument in the following manner:

> Evolution . . . I define as a process of increasing differentiation and complexity of organization that endows the . . . unit in question . . . with greater capacity to adapt to its environment . . . I do not assume that evolution is inevitable, irreversible, or must follow any single particular course . . . What I mean is nothing metaphysical but the simple empirical generalization that more complex forms develop from less complex forms. (Bellah 1970:21)

Strictly interpreted, this seems to mean something like the following. If form B succeeds form A, there are three possibilities: 1) form B is more complex and more adaptive, in which case evolution has occurred; 2) form A is more complex and adaptive, in which case reversal has occurred; 3) (not stated but implied) form B, though different, is of the same order of complexity and adaptivity, in which case nothing has occurred in evolutionary terms.

But Bellah has not, of course, brought us here to hear such banal and colorless stuff and it soon becomes clear that not all these possibilities are equally likely, for he goes on to elaborate "for heuristic purposes" a scheme of five "stages" (primitive, archaic, historic, early modern, modern) which march along in succession as surely as did the "stages" of the nineteenth-century evolutionists. This scheme, he assures us, is not to be a "Procrustean bed," but then he likens its logic to that involved in conceptualizing the stages of personality development! (1970:25) This surely gives the game away, for in every theory of personality development of which I am aware, personalities which regress or remain in the same stage for more than a certain period are regarded as pathological. Is Bellah willing to follow the "logic" to that conclusion? In principle, he seems to deny it,[1] but his remarks about the "regressive" nature of Karl Barth's theology in the "modern stage" (1970:41)[2] lead one to the reluctant conclusion that he takes the analogy between personality development and sociocultural history seriously — as seriously as other evolutionists have taken the analogy between such history and (misunderstood) organic evolution.

I will give one other example (among many) of the Procrustean bed at work, despite its creator's protestations to the contrary: The "historic religions are characterized above all by religious rejection of the world . . . an extremely negative evaluation of man and society and the exaltation of another realm of reality as alone true and infinitely valuable" (Bellah 1970:22). Now there may be some insight to be derived from a formulation which, through the common element of "salvation," casts together Hellenic Greece, Buddhism, Hinduism, Judaism, early Christianity and Islam, but the degrees and kinds of "world rejection" involved in these various religious systems seem to me to vary so widely as to render that insight very thin indeed.

   1. "I hope it is clear that a complex and differentiated religious symbolization is not therefore a better or truer or more beautiful one than a compact religious symbolization" (Bellah 1970:22).
   2. An alternative interpretation of Barth's "neo-orthodox" theology as a response to the then prevailing "liberal theology," and one which I prefer, is that it represents a recurrent phenomenon in the Christian and other "historic" traditions, namely a "returning to the sources" in the face of a sense that faith has conceded too much to secular culture. But here, I believe, both Bellah and I are simply expressing preferences; I find no basis in evolutionary or other social scientific interpretation for a decision between us.

Finally, despite his frequently dolorous tone in this and other essays, Bellah remains incurably optimistic about the future: "Yet the very (modern) situation which has been characterized as one of the collapse of meaning and the failure of moral standards can also, and I would argue more fruitfully, be viewed as one offering unprecedented opportunities for creative innovation in every sphere of human action" (1970:44). No recognition of the possibility of stasis or reversal here!

I do not wish to belittle Bellah's work on religion for I have learned much from his insights into particular forms of religious thought and action. I do wish to suggest that evolutionary thinking has contributed little to those insights — indeed that it has, if anything, constricted them and inhibited their flowering.

Parsons himself also remains optimistic; he remains confident of the development of ever higher levels of "generalized adaptive capacity" through "higher levels of cybernetic control." By this, I assume he means an enlarged capacity to cope through the development of an increased ability to create, store, retrieve and manipulate cultural information, which then feeds back into more adaptive technological, social and ecological arrangements (Parsons 1966:5-29). Armed with this conviction, he is "relatively optimistic" (Parsons 1971:141) about the future.

For a profound admirer of Parsons' great synthesis of the "voluntaristic theory of action" as presented in his earlier (1937) work, there is deep irony in this retreat to positivistic optimism about the future. For surely nothing could be less conducive to "generalized adaptive capacity" in our time than certainty, or even "conviction," about our future course. In a world threatened by nuclear and demographic disaster, nothing could be more absurd. Skepticism is surely the more "adaptive" attitude. What evolutionists seem to forget is that man's earlier biocultural history has condemned him (or blessed him, as you like) with the necessity of managing his affairs through his mind, not his genes. The mind is of course cultural, but culture is not a "mechanism"; it must be recreated, whether in old or new forms, in every generation.

Let me be clear: *Of course* adaptive capacity is a crucial aspect of the human condition. It is the enduring achievement of the evolutionary, "materialist" tradition in social thought to have drawn this to our attention. It is only when adaptivity comes to be seen as the single critical aspect of sociocultural change that this mode of thought becomes a prison. For biologists, such a view is useful; for them, "evolution" *is* the history of adaptation. It is, of course, *possible* to view men in the same light, but then the logical conclusion must be accepted: all talk of "meaningful," "intentional" action is absurd.

Man, in Parsons' 1937 formulation, was conditioned by "human heredity and nonhuman environment"; he acted within the constraints of historically given cultures and societies. But for all this he remained a true intentional actor, capable in some meaningful degree of taking all those conditioning and constraining elements in his situation into his own hands — and into his mind — and creating, in some degree, his own future. Today's Parsonian man has become a component in a marvelously intricate sociocultural super-computer, programmed by God, Fate or Evolution for a history which is inexorably predetermined and hence, ultimately, meaningless. If we were to take these ideas seriously, we would place ourselves in precisely the predicament of Max Weber's predestinarian Calvinists in *The Protestant Ethic and the Spirit of Capitalism:* unable to influence our fate, we should be obliged nevertheless to think and act as if we could in order to render our situation meaningful, and hence tolerable (Weber 1958:111).

Perhaps we do need certainty about the future of man on earth, much as our ancestors required certainty about the fate of their souls. I for one do not accept this, with regard to either ourselves or our ancestors. I shall shortly suggest what I regard as a better solution for ourselves. I also think it can be shown that, in the long sweep of the Christian tradition (not to speak of other traditions), both before and after Calvin, it has been much commoner to regard the problem of the fate of the soul in the face of an omnipotent God who also imposes freedom to choose as a mystery requiring faith, not a logical puzzle to be solved. But if we do require certainty, then let us be clear about the sort of enterprise we are engaged in.

Theories of historical inevitability do not always take an evolutionary form — that is to say, a form which stresses directional development from within. Some writers stress the diffusion or borrowing of elements from other societies. For example, there is Clark Kerr's lyrical statement of the inevitability of industrialization:

> . . . for industrialism is a great magnet which is drawing all human life to it and ordering the orientation of this life. Whether a society has been patrilineal or matrilineal, whether based upon tribal or family ownership of land, whether responding to the Protestant ethic or the Bantu ethic, or whether it goes through a prior commercial revolution or not, it ends up following the logic of industrialism . . . the present can be penetrated from the vantage–point of the future because the motto of the future is *e pluribus unum* and *unum* (the new industrial society) is fairly well–known. (Kerr 1960:348-50)

Many citizens of "developing nations" I know would be happy to learn that the industrialization of their countries is inevitable. For good or ill, however, such assurance cannot be given, for the successful borrowing of the technology and sociocultural organization of industrial production is no more certain than their development from within.

In an excellent recent discussion of "the state of the art" of

"social forecasting" in which he reviews many past failures of
social prophecy, Otis Dudley Duncan presents an alternative,
and to my mind much more adequate, statement of the
relationship between social science and historical understanding than that propounded by the seers of evolution and diffusion:

> As ingredients of our forecasts we will, with increasing
> methodological sophistication, continue to prepare projections,
> trend extrapolations, model simulations and developmental
> constructs so as to provide as broad an array as may be useful of
> the logically possible pathways to hypothetical futures . . . .
> There will be no pretense that we can gradually move forward to
> the perfection of methods of anticipating what will actually occur,
> for such perfectibility is not logically possible, aesthetically
> appealing or morally inspiring. What we may hope to improve, if
> not perfect, is our sense of responsibility for making known the im-
> plications of our knowledge. (Duncan 1939:115)

Clearly many excellent minds *do* find the prophetic vision
aesthetically appealing and morally inspiring, but Duncan is
surely right about its logical weakness.

But let us return, now, after a rather wide detour. All this
clearly has implications for our thinking about what Edward
Shils has called the "promethean urge to Modernity" in
contemporary states:

> There are very few states today which do not aspire to modernity.
> The day of rulers who were indifferent to the archaism of the
> society which they governed has almost disappeared. The leaders
> of nearly every state — both the old established states as well as the
> new states of Asia and Africa — feel a pressing necessity of es-
> pousing policies which will bring them well within the circle of
> modernity. Much of the opposition which they encounter among
> their politically interested countrymen contends that they are not
> modern enough. Many traditionalists are constrained to assert
> that only by cleaving to the essence of older traditions can a
> genuine and stable modernity be attained. (Shils 1962:7)

Now what is this "modernity" of which so much has been made recently by social scientists, especially those concerned with the affairs of the Third World? One dictionary sense of the term has it synonymous with "contemporary" or "present-day." What was "modern" a century and a half ago — the "spinning jenny," for example — is now "archaic," or even "primitive." But this is clearly not what Shils and others mean when they speak of the modernization of societies and cultures. "Among the elites of the new states," Shils writes, "'modern' means dynamic, concerned with the people, democratic and equalitarian, scientific, economically advanced, sovereign and influential" (1962:7). Modernity in this sense does not mean contemporaneity; rather it is a construct in the minds of persons who aspire to something different from and, as they see it, better than the present. It is a list of collective goals, a multifaceted macrosociocultural project.

But from what source does this conception or construct derive? How is it formed in the minds of those who possess and make ideological use of it in summoning themselves and their people to action? How do social scientists arrive at, and make use of, the concept of modernity in their efforts to grasp processes of sociocultural change in contemporary nation–states?

It is just here that theories of historical inevitability — evolutionary theories — diverge from what we may call, following the early Parsons, voluntaristic–historical ones. For those who think about these matters in an evolutionary or diffusionist mode, modernization is an immanent, ineluctable process, modernity a new, "emergent stage" — whether the "mechanism" is dissonance among society, culture and personality (Kirsch and Peacock) or the class struggle (Marx) or selection toward greater generalized adaptivity (Parsons, White), or the logic of technology and institutions (Kerr). But the inevitability which this language suggests is belied by the hortatory rhetoric which often accompanies it. Leaders who speak in terms of being "on the side of history" do so in order to inspire their people to efforts which they recognize to be far from inevitable, while social scientists who write about historical or evolutionary "laws" see themselves as providing the knowledge to make the operation of those laws both more certain and less painful. These concessions to the role of effort and thought represent a recognition, however partial and distorted, of the force of the voluntaristic view that history is made by men in groups, finding themselves in situations created by their predecessors and acting in ways that will create new situations for their successors. Both actors in history and those who seek to understand them may — indeed must — create conceptual constructs which encapsulate, and even reify, their grasp of social situations, past, present and hypothetical future. It is important, though, that these constructs be recognized for the creations of the human mind that they actually are and that they not be mistaken for concrete historical reality.

The contemporary notion of modernity as a necessary historical stage or condition is the product of both ideologists' and social scientists' efforts to grasp, and orient themselves to, a particular situation which has two characteristics: 1) that there exists among countries a very unequal distribution of those qualities listed by Edward Shils — dynamism, equality, democracy, knowledge, autonomy and influence; and, 2) equally important, one in which there is a unprecedentedly world–wide and general *perception* of this inequality. The rise, in the eighteenth and nineteenth centuries, of Western Europe and North America to almost unchallenged world ascendancy presented a conceptual challenge all around. In the West it produced a sense of exhilaration which set ideologists to talking of "manifest destiny" and the "white man's burden" and intellectuals to devising laws of history. Whether they found the contemporary consummation grim, as did Marx and Engels, or glorious, as did Spencer and Sumner, all agreed that the West of the age of high capitalism and imperialism represented the pattern for the rest of mankind as surely as mankind as a whole represented the culmination of God's or nature's biological creation. A few moralists and pessimistic philosophers aside, Left and Right joined in celebrating Western industrial civilization as a universal exemplar and as a solvent of traditional diversity. Although he, of course, saw the more remote future differently, Marx was as enthusiastic a Westernizer, intellectually, as Herbert Spencer. And so overwhelming was the Western ascendancy in power and wealth that non-Western peoples — or at least their leaders — rather generally saw the situation in the same light: the key to participation in this new wealth and power lay in Westernization, in borrowing from the West, even in becoming Western. As we have seen, this latter became, and remains, the dominant view in Turkey.

However, other things were happening, too. The Japanese defeat of Russia in 1905 drew world-wide attention to a people who had borrowed massively from Western science, technology and governmental organization but who remained unmistakably themselves in other, quite fundamental, respects.[3] All throughout the non-Western world, similar processes were soon in evidence. In 1938 Kabaka Daudi Cwa of Buganda addressed the youth of his country in the following terms:

3. It is a good index of the ambivalence of the Turkish commitment to "Westernization" that Turks find the Japanese example extremely fascinating. A Turkish translation of Ruth Benedict's *The Chrysanthemum and the Sword* is popular among intellectuals.

I have considered it my duty . . . to strongly warn all members of the present generation of young Baganda that while they are legitimately entitled to strive to acquire education and civilization, they should also take very great care that (these) do not destroy their inherited customs and traditions, which in my view are quite as good as those found in Western civilized countries and which only require developing and remodeling where necessary. (Kaizi 1948:246)

I heard such sentiments expressed by many young, educated Baganda and Basoga during the early 1950s. Particularly common was the notion that "we must industrialize without experiencing the horrors of the industrial revolution in Europe," about which they had learned at school. So that when, following the Second World War, the Third World nations were able to assert their independence of at least formal Western political domination, this was accompanied by an assertion of separate sociocultural identity as well, and by a search for alternative paths to the future.

As ideology, the idea of "modernity" often expresses this declaration of independence, as over against "Westernization." In social science it represents a recognition that progress toward greater wealth, knowledge and influence does not, and in fact cannot, involve a simple replication of Western European, American — or indeed Soviet or Japanese — experience, for, quite aside from the continuing influence of distinct local tradition, becoming "modern" in the third quarter of the twentieth century is a very different thing from what it was fifty or a hundred years ago. Industrializing is different in a world whose international economy is dominated by the already industrialized. It is different in a world in which citizens expect, and are encouraged to expect, of their governments kinds of services and degrees of political participation that would have horrified the entrepreneurs and politicians of early industrial Europe and America.

While the new states that came into being after the Second
World War were, and for the most part remain, backward
economically, they were born "modern" in a number of important respects. They generally began life with constitutions
that encouraged both populistic politics and a high demand for
benefits from the state. However much these things might be
clothed in traditional cultural idiom, and however much older
social forms might be made use of, universal suffrage, trade
unions, mass communications, widespread public education
and the capacity to convert science to technology for the
amelioration of life's miseries were expected of the new
governments. Unfortunately, these governments too frequently were ones whose revenues were small, whose legitimacy,
and hence authority, were often precarious and whose in-
capacity to satisfy impossible popular demands left them with
little choice but to act to reduce the demands to manageable
proportions. Some of these states have been able to create and
maintain authority based upon some combination of
traditional legitimacy and anti–imperialist charisma; others
have been able to avoid the politicization of some substantial
part of their population, and thus to maintain themselves while
making some headway economically; but others have found
that the very effort to mobilize their people for material
progress simply further dissolves the routine structures of
everyday life which form the indispensable background and
platform for constructive effort. Many have thus fallen into
political disorder and then into military rule, or authoritarian
rule backed by military force. For the one aspect of
"modernity" that seems most easily borrowed is sufficient
military organization and technology to cow unarmed
civilians.

When the states of Western Europe and North America were
young, "modernity" as an explicitly conceptualized goal did

not, in the nature of the case, exist, for they themselves were in the process of creating, unselfconsciously and gradually, the sort of sociocultural life from which that goal could be abstracted only later on. They of course had goals — to be richer and more powerful, particularly in relation to each other — but they were no more able to foresee their overweening world dominance than are we, still precariously dominant, able to discern through the present murk whatever future lies ahead of us. It is the peculiar burden of the leaders of the Third World that they and their people see all too clearly, in the shape of the Western societies and Japan, the condition — at least the material condition — to which they aspire, while lacking the means and conditions to bring the goal nearer or even, in many cases, to prevent it from receding, for the societies that presently lead the race are themselves forever changing. It is uncomfortable to realize that the leaders of most of the world's states can imagine nothing sweeter than to have their air and water fouled by the industrial pollution whose elimination has become a leading public issue in Western Europe and the United States — for that would mean economic progress. It is equally uncomfortable to recognize how fragile is the civility of even the most powerful and prosperous states, how little, really, economic progress has contributed to their capacity to maintain the precarious balance between unity and differentiation — between consensus and freedom — that popular government requires.

Let me sum up, now, in a preliminary way. While human sociocultural history, like biological history, involves processes which are general and predictable, given specific conditions, its actual course involves an immensely complex interplay of processes, sociocultural and ecological, which is, in its full concreteness, unpredictable and nonrepeatable. In addition, the processes of sociocultural history, unlike those of the biological sort, involve a measure of meaning–creation and of choice which renders it even less inevitable. Human history is thus in a double sense open ended.

# five

# IMPLICATIONS,
# THEORETICAL
# AND PRACTICAL

We must study, we must investigate, we must attempt to solve; and the utmost the world can demand is, not lack of human interest and moral conviction, but rather the heart-quality of fairness, and an earnest desire for the truth despite its possible unpleasantness.

W.E.B. DUBOIS, 1899

Having concluded that neither social anthropology nor social science in general can predict the outcome of contemporary nation-states' struggles with their problems, I nevertheless revert, following Duncan, to the more modest suggestion that the social sciences, in proper conjunction with other fields of study, *can* contribute to an *understanding* of these problems and hence, perhaps, to the capacity for intelligent self-direction.

The most important quality required of such a social science, including social anthropology, is that its conceptual apparatus avoid the current enthusiasm for closed systems, for such conceptualizations are incompatible with the open-endedness of history. There is, of course, a sense in which any scientific theory must, at the most abstract level, seek logical closure. It must seek orderliness and internal consistency. There are a good many elegant (in this sense) theories and models in the social sciences, particularly in economics, linguistics, demography and some fields of psychology. The more plausible of them, however, seem to have in common a degree of abstraction from the experienced flow of sociocultural life that makes them useful only in combination with each other, or with innumerable *ceteris paribus* caveats, for the analysis of the life of nation–states, or of that of their constituent microcosms, which is the special domain of social anthropology. The concepts available to us for this purpose are not, I suggest, most usefully viewed as closed conceptual systems for the additional reason that what we are after here is understanding on a rather lower level of abstraction — understanding of something much closer to wide–awake, practical, common sense experience. Concepts such as "society," "culture," and "personality," and the subconcepts that cluster in and around them, such as "politics," "religion," or "ego identity," are of course abstractions, but they are abstractions of a rather low order, far better suited to the analysis of particular historical or biographical situations than to the construction of sets of logically interrelated propositions. Or rather I should perhaps say that when built into tightly integrated conceptual constructions, they generally produce rather disappointing results.

An example will perhaps help clarify what I mean. Max Gluckman, more than any other writer, at least among social anthropologists, has carried the idea of a society as an integrated system to its logical conclusion. In his book *Politics, Law and Ritual in Tribal Societies* (1965:279) he asserts: "Anthropologists analyse a society as if it were in a state of equilibrium" (see also Gluckman and Devons 1964). "Equilibrium," he goes on to say, "is the tendency of a system to return after disturbance to its previous state" (1965:279). Now no sociologist or social anthropologist would wish to deny that the idea of society as a system of interrelated elements has proved stimulating, or indeed that the idea of equilibrium is not a useful extension of it. But Gluckman seems to suggest that these ideas by themselves make up an adequate view of society and he ends by defeating his own purposes. For he is also interested in "radical change," change which breaks through, or goes beyond, equilibrium–restoring processes. But, he says, "the sources of radical change escape [social anthropological] analysis . . . perhaps . . . because [it] aims to be scientific" (1965:286). The best the social anthropologist can do is to analyze societies as equilibrium systems at successive points in time and fill in the gaps with narrative.

The reason Gluckman is forced to relegate to narrative what he clearly wishes he could analyze "scientifically" is that he identifies scientific inquiry with conceptualization in terms of closed (in the sense of equilibrium–maintaining) systems. That part of experience not captured by the equilibrium model is, in these terms, outside the reach of science. However, if one understands "science" more broadly to embrace inquiry other than that based upon analogies with organismic biology or cybernetics, then this is not necessarily so. Societies ought not be be viewed as closed systems if this way of proceeding hinders us from inquiring into those matters which we most want to understand. Culture, too, may be treated as a closed system — a "logically integrated whole" — but at the expense of letting slip through our fingers some of its most interesting features: tension, ambiguity, contradiction, syncretism and the like. Much "structuralist" analysis of culture seems to me to be open to this objection.

It is simply not the case that science, including social science, lacks conceptual tools for analyzing processes of change in kind, as contrasted with structures and equilibrating or homeostatic processes. There is no doubt a tendency toward a restoration of order, a tendency rooted in the discomfort of living in sociocultural disorder (the feeling of betrayal resulting from the sense of obligations unfulfilled, the feeling of disorientation that occurs when one's map of the world fails to guide). But a degree of disorder is also "normal" precisely because the persons and groups that make up human communities are constantly, if at very different rates, engaged in the "creative destruction" of existing order through the establishment of new kinds of social ties and novel ideas. W.I. Thomas (1917) recognized this in a preliminary way when he listed "the desire for new experience" among his "four wishes." Max Weber made more pointed use of it in his notions of "charisma" and of "rationalization" within cultural traditions.[1] A recognition of the pervasiveness of such processes, along with that of equilibrium–restoring ones, must make us skeptical of the idea of a society or culture as a "boundary–maintaining system."

In saying all this, I am not arguing for the primacy in social science generally or in social anthropology of unmediated perception — a kind of radical empiricism — for that kind of direct encounter with the world is, in my view, not possible. Rather I am opting for a degree of conceptual eclecticism which seems to be necessary to the understanding of particular human situations, microcosmic, macrocosmic or of any scale in between. For I simply do care more for an ability to understand the situation of the Baganda or that of the people of Edremit than I do for the elegance of conceptual constructs as such. Again, *theoria* and *praxis* are of course complementary, both in everyday life and (in a more explicit way), in scientific life. If, however, one cares more for the particular human community in its particular situation, then the aesthetic pleasures of enveloping it in one or another closed system of analysis must yield, in some degree, to the more "practical"

---

1. In his *Sociology of Religion* (1963) and in his separate studies of China, India, ancient Judaism and Protestant Christianity.

task of understanding also those elements in the situation not captured by that system. Conversely, if one cares more for theoretical elegance or aesthetic closure, one must give up a measure of practical relevance. This, too, involves a choice among values and I do not presume to call it inferior to the one I have made — or perhaps the one to which I am consigned by my own nature.

"Practical relevance" does not, or need not, mean immediate applicability to problems of public policy, though it may, of course, mean that. Here I mean by it something rather broader: a style of inquiry which enhances our capacity to understand the hopes and fears, the triumphs and tragedies of human communities in their historical settings and hence contributes to our own and others' wisdom as citizens of the nation and the world. If we seek this sort of understanding, we will do well to inform our more abstract analyses with a measure of common sense.

Common sense experience tells us that change is pervasive. It also tells us that much of life, both personal and collective, is routine, repetitive and fixed. Do we wish to understand change — even "radical" change — and not merely experience it, in order that we may accelerate, guide or prevent it? Do we wish to establish or break out of routine and conformity and to understand others' efforts to do so? Let us then fashion our tools accordingly, making use of social science abstractions and of analogies from other sciences when they serve our scientific purposes and dropping them when they do not. Let us develop what John Dewey, if he were alive today and aware of our concerns, might call a "social anthropology of experience" — a social anthropology true to our experience as persons and to our experience as enquirers attempting to understand others' experience. This does not mean abandoning social anthropology as we have known it but merely subjecting it to the test of usefulness for our purposes and modifying it accordingly.

In my view, the major concepts that have become conventional in the subject, "society," "culture," and "personality," have served us well and can serve us better, but not if we view them as closed systems, either severally or taken together, and not if we view them each in isolation. Talcott Parsons was, I believe, on the right track when he suggested in 1937 that at the heart of an adequate social science must lie a conception of the project-pursuing actor, acting individually or in concert with others, constrained and guided by his organism, his organized personality, his ecological setting, his encoded culture and his network of social relations, but yet "free" enough to "intend" and "attempt," to "succeed" or "fail." (The language here is not strictly that of *The Structure of Social Action,* but rather an up-dating of it which remains within its spirit. The updating is mine, not Parsons'; the upshot (as we have seen) is quite different from that of the later work which he himself views as the proper development of his ideas.)

*Organism*: The evidence thus far seems to weigh against the view that the problem of "basic human nature" — the problem of what all persons share as human animals — can be abandoned as irrelevant to social science. Margaret Mead's assertion that while human fatherhood is a social invention, human motherhood rests upon continuities in primate evolution (1949) suggests an asymmetry in the plasticity of sex roles which, at the very least, remains to be further explored. So also do notions about the constraining influence of a host of other "biological factors," ranging from ageing to the psychology of perception. The actor as organism is neither constant nor infinitely malleable. At the same time the project of medical science to make him more malleable "on purpose" is certainly neither futile nor meaningless (though we may regard such projects as variously benign or horrifying). The organism is an object of, and participant in, action as well as a constraint upon it.

*Personality*: Social anthropology cannot do without a concept of the actor as person, either as typical or as individual person, either as typical or particular complex of organism and sociocultural conditioning which experiments and experiences in both typical and idiosyncratic ways. Indeed, the very notion of the voluntaristic actor implies a measure of individuality in Everyman. And every social anthropologist, in the course of his work, comes upon persons, either within the immediate microcosms with which he is directly concerned or in the larger macrocosmic environment, whose individuality has had profound consequences for their milieux. There is a sense in which one cannot understand the present–day Baganda without understanding Mukabya Mutesa I, the king who ruled them in the crucial third quarter of the nineteenth century, during the initial phase of their fateful encounter with Europe. Since the data in this instance are severely limited there remain substantial lacunae in our understanding of the Ganda experience which will probably never be filled. Where materials are richer, as in the case of Mustafa Kemal, the possibilities are of course much greater. Erik Erikson has shown what can be done in his psycho–sociocultural biographies of Luther (1962) and Gandhi (1969). The fascination which the personality of Atatürk holds for both Turks and students of modern Turkey, including the fascination with his strange sexual life (strange to Turks, as well as to Europeans and Americans) does not, or need not, represent either hero–worship or prurient curiosity; for that particular blending of volcanic organismic energy, sociocultural formation and political intelligence deeply influenced one of the twentieth century's more arresting experiences in nation–statehood. Among other things, the "extraordinary man" — heroic or demonic (usually both) — gives us an interpretation of his sociocultural world which, while inevitably self-serving, is inevitably informative as well.

*Ecology*: Neither can social anthropology dispense with the idea of the environment as an open system involving the interaction of the sociocultural actors, both individual and collective, with nonhuman nature in their pursuit of subsistence and, beyond subsistence, of scarce resources toward whatever ends. Laying aside the current enthusiasm for the ecological perspective as ideology or master science, such a perspective remains essential as a means of conceptualizing crucial aspects of the setting of sociocultural action, including space and time, as well as what are conventionally called "natural resources" and the products of human artifice.

But, of course, the most prominent among social anthropology's conceptual tools are the notions of "society" and "culture." The first has been built up from reflection upon the common-sense experience of interpersonal mutual expectation (satisfied or frustrated), from the observation that human projects involve cooperation and competition. The second, "culture," rests upon the experience of common meaning mediated by symbols — upon the experienced capacity for "intersubjectivity." So much of the discussion of these concepts has been muddled by the tendency to treat society and culture as different *things* that I have very often in these lectures preferred to use the compound "sociocultural" instead to emphasize the concretely inextricable interconnectedness of meaning and social interaction. Nevertheless, there remains a useful analytic distinction on both the individual and the collective level between theory and practice — between putting our thoughts in order and putting our affairs in order — even though both must be involved in social encounter.[2] Ex-

2. Richard J. Bernstein provides an excellent discussion of several philosophical approaches to this relationship in his *Praxis and Action* (1971).

perience, both individual and collective, also involves meaningful encounter with phenomena other than persons, although of course not intersubjective encounter. Such encounter, like the interpersonal sort, may involve not only recognition but also interpretation and reinterpretation, although only insofar as such experience is communicable and communicated through shared symbols does it become cultural.

One of Max Weber's greatest services to social science was to show us how to recognize and work with the interaction of the logic of culture and that of institutionalized mutual expectation in human experience. Sociocultural macrocosms — "societies" — he saw as made up of many culture–bearing and culture–creating collectivities, pursuing purposes, both in cooperation and in conflict, purposes which they more and less explicitly revise and reconceptualize as they encounter social consequences and work through the logic of their ideas and ideals. He was very much the successor to Marx; his model was the medieval European "estate" or status group, though he extended it beyond such society–wide strata to such groups as lawyers, priests and even musicians. In each case he teased out the complex interrelatedness between "ideal" and "material" interests: the collectivity pursues its material interests in the light of cultural beliefs and values that legitimate them,[3] thus, in Tom Lehrer's deathless phrase "doing well by doing good." But what Tom Lehrer meant simply as a jab at moral pretension, Weber recognized as inherent in every human enterprise.

The example that I find most convincing to modern materialists, who find it difficult to credit Weber's assertion that the logic of Calvinist theology played a significant role in the growth of bourgeois capitalist economic organization, is not one of Weber's but rather that of modern science as

3. The most fully worked–out of Weber's studies on this theme is of course *The Protestant Ethic* (1958) though he applied it much more widely.

analyzed by Thomas Kuhn in his *The Structure of Scientific Revolutions* (1963). Kuhn's scientists, are bound together in a common enterprise which has its own social organization and "material base." They seek personal and collective recognition through successful performance in working out the logical implications of scientific "paradigms" — cultural constructions which order their tasks — and thus, occasionally, produce results like $e = mc^2$ whose material and social consequences are all too apparent.[4]

The nation–state, too, is a continuing project, involving collective experiment and experience. It is also an arena for a multitude of lesser projects, of many kinds and on many levels. The central problem of the nation–state, which is to say the central problem for its people and their leaders, is to maintain a reasonable balance between the national project and those projects of lesser scale, and, of course, a reasonable degree of order among the lesser projects as well. The smaller–scale projects are sometimes the vanguard of the national experience. Through them, the nation may experiment with ideas and ideals, with organization and the commitment of resources, without putting the national project at unnecessary risk, and without demanding of the citizens at large a constricting and distracting overparticipation in the nation — that is, nationalist excitement. This latter is important, for the relative tranquility of the microcosmic lives of the citizens, most of the time, is a necessary condition for their creative and satisfying conduct of the smaller–scale, mostly routine, projects — familial, occupational, identity–creating and simple, harmless pleasure–pursuing. These smaller–scale projects serve to make up lives sufficiently rewarding and untroubled so that the in-

---

4. All the above aspects of the conduct of science are nicely illustrated by James Watson's *The Double Helix: A Personal Account of the Discovery of the Structure of DNA* (1968).

dividuals may occasionally give their intelligent attention to the special arts of the citizen — to the conduct of the national project and to the assessment of the place of their own smaller–scale projects within it.

All this requires creative and sensitive leadership at all levels — leadership which combines with imagination a regard for civil relations among citizens and groups of citizens. To say this is not to propose a pat formula for political virtue; leadership must begin with things as they are — with societies in their particular situations — and these situations vary enormously, as the Turkish and East African ventures in nation–statehood show. Atatürk's Turkey invited a kind of revolutionary leadership to fend off a palpable external threat and to create out of the ruins of a discredited and demoralized empire a new national identity which could form a basis for civic self–respect.

As the Turkish Republic reaches its fiftieth birthday (1973), it seems correct to say that he and those who followed him succeeded to a remarkable degree (measured by the magnitude of the task) in creating a common Turkish citizenship capable of accommodating in a civil manner a much greater degree of sociocultural differentiation, which is to say a much greater scope for the individual and collective projects at all levels of Turkish society. The general acceptance of the republic's legitimacy, together with what citizens, looking back at their individual and collective experience, speak of with appreciation as the growth of a less constricting social order — a greater freedom to choose — testifies to this success.

At the same time, Atatürk's leadership deepened the tension between religious and secular culture — a tension which has occasionally broken out into violent incivility — and few indeed among his heirs have had the imagination to attempt the ideological synthesis necessary to reduce this source of incivility. This failure has been particularly marked among intellectuals, although there has also developed a body of practicing parliamentary politicians increasingly capable of supporting such a synthesis. Less peculiar to Turkey are the new tensions arising from economic growth and differentiation.

Finally, the prominence of the military in the republic, a prominence inherited from the empire, reinforced by the struggle for national survival and stimulated again by Turkey's post–Second World War alliance with the United States and NATO, has constituted a standing threat of authoritarianism in response to civil disorder. Whether or not the threat from the Soviet Union was sufficient to require a large military establishment armed with modern weapons, I do not know. I am inclined to think it was, but the consequences for internal politics are nevertheless real. The generals have sometimes acted with great restraint in support of civil politics; at other times they have openly threatened the civil political order. At this point in the Turkish experiment in nation–statehood one can only say that democracy lives, if somewhat precariously.

East Africa is the scene of not one but several ventures in nation–statehood. Each is being played out within some particular variation on the East African setting, with its pattern of cross–cutting ethnic, religious, economic and political ties and interests. All are "artificial" nations born of the European scramble for colonies. Fifteen years ago all were poor, even by Turkish standards, and hence the primary task of leadership was to manage both primordial diversity and diversity of economic situation in the interest of development.

Of course there were significant differences among the incipient states and their societies. Zanzibar was the most compact and the most homogeneous religiously, but also the most divided by class interests. Uganda seemed to possess the highest level of general civility, though the problem of Buganda versus the rest lurked ominously in the wings. Kenya, on the other hand, with its history of racial tension culminating in the violence of the Mau Mau period, seemed to possess the least civility and the greatest potentiality for disorder. And Tanganyika was simply the poorest and most politically backward of the lot, although ethnic atomization and possession of a common lingua franca reduced the likelihood of primordial conflict. These were my own impressions at the time.

The brief post–independence civic histories of these states are not, I believe, explicable on the basis of the differences I have outlined, although they have, of course, been shaped by them. The two nations that have suffered the most violence and authoritarianism — Uganda and Zanzibar — were in many ways those best fitted to avoid such misfortunes. Kenya's and Tanzania's greater success, thus far, in avoiding them must, I think, be attributed at least in part to more devoted and intelligent leadership. Jomo Kenyatta, the charismatic anti-imperialist turned shrewd machine politician, and Julius Nyerere, the high–minded exemplar turned subtle democratic centralist, have, each in his own way, cared deeply and thought creatively about preserving civility within their respective situations. Liberal parliamentary democracy does not, at present, exist within any of the East African states, but the actions of some leaders have nurtured to a greater extent the indigenous grass–roots civility which is friendly to the growth of greater democracy; those of others have served to erode it. The slackening provision of economic support by the developed nations — particularly the United States — has not helped matters.

* * * * *

I am aware that much of what I have said here has the ring of civic platitude. But then, I have emphasized throughout the close relationship — not the identity, but the close relationship — of social anthropological understanding to that of wide–awake common sense, of which civility is a dimension. For what is at issue here is the very practical problem of living within the nation–state until some other form of common life supersedes it. My concentration upon the practical does not imply a hostility to the freer flights of theorizing as such or to a concern with matters quite unpractical and nonpolitical. Social science can improve upon common sense by subjecting it to self–conscious scrutiny, thereby opening its presuppositions to intelligent choice. Even the more abstract formulations of social science have occasionally added substantially to our insight into the human situation. But as a caution against *hubris* — a common social scientific vice — it is worth recalling that these "great ideas" have often had morally ambiguous consequences, as perhaps all useful knowledge does.

For example, the utilitarian theory of social action, which dominated much of social thought from the time of Hobbes until well into the nineteenth century, was enormously creative and successful. The abstraction of the means–ends calculus from the rest of sociocultural life produced economics, both theoretical and applied, as well as important segments of psychology, sociology and political science. Insofar as it passed into popular culture and into public policy, it played an important role in the economic burgeoning of the West. But it also produced tragedy that more traditional, common–sense morality might have avoided.

Cecil Woodham–Smith has written of the utilitarians who dominated the British treasury at the time of the great Irish potato famine:

Adherence to the doctrine of *laissez–faire* was carried to such a length that in the midst of one of the great famines of history the government was perpetually nervous of being too good to Ireland and of corrupting the Irish people by kindness, and so stifling the virtues of self-reliance and industry. (1962:410-11)

The men of the treasury were excellent utilitarian economists, but they were also, in a phrase of Saul Bellow's, "high I.Q. morons." Perhaps simple prejudice against the Irish without the aid of utilitarian doctrine would in any case have overcome the government's common-sense moral duty to feed starving people for whom it was responsible. Then again it might not, for a century and a quarter later the same sort of thinking remains influential in the world's richest and most powerful nation-state.

# REFERENCES

Balcıoğlu, Tahir Harimi
  1937 *Tahrite Edremit Şehri (The City of Edremit in History)*. Balıkesir: Vilayet Matbaası.
Bartlett, C.A.
  1936 *Statistics of the Zanzibar Protectorate, 1898-1935*. Zanzibar: Government Printer.
Batutta, Ibn
  1962 *The Travels of Ibn Batutta*. Cambridge: Hakluyt Society, Second Series, No. 117.
Bellah, Robert N.
  1957 *Tokugawa Religion*. Glencoe: The Free Press.
  1970 *Beyond Belief: Essays on Religion in a Post-Traditional World*. New York: Harper and Row.
Berger, Peter, and Thomas Luckman
  1966 *The Social Construction of Reality*. New York: Doubleday.
Bernstein, Richard J.
  1971 *Praxis and Action*. Philadelphia: University of Pennsylvania Press.
de Jouvenel, Bertrand
  1957 *Sovereignty: An Inquiry into the Political Good*. Cambridge: Cambridge University Press.
Derin, Naci
  1968 *Yaşadığımız Çevre: Edremit (Edremit: The Environment in which We Live)*. İzmir: Yeniyol Matbaası.
Dobzhansky, Theodosius
  1962 *Mankind Evolving*. New Haven: Yale University Press.

159

Dubois, W.E.B.
  1899 *The Philadelphia Negro*. New York: Schocken Books, 1967.
Duncan, Otis Dudley
  1939 "Social Forecasting: The State of the Art." *The Public Interest* 17 (fall):88-118.
Ecevit, Bülent
  1966 *Ortanin Solu (Left of Center)*. Ankara: Kim Yayınları.
el Zein, Abdul Hamid
  in press *The Golden Meadow*. Evanston: Northwestern University Press.
Erer, Tekin
  1965 *Yassıada ve Sonrası (Yassıada and Its Sequel)*. İstanbul: Rek-Tur Kitap Servisi.
Erikson, Erik H.
  1962 *Young Man Luther*. New York: Norton.
  1969 *Gandhi's Truth: On the Origins of Militant Non-Violence*. New York: Norton.
Fallers, L.A.
  1964 (Ed.) *The King's Men: Authority and Status in Buganda on the Eve of Independence*. London: Oxford University Press on Behalf of the East African Institute of Social Research.
  1969 *Law Without Precedent: Legal Ideas in Action in the Courts of Colonial Busoga*. Chicago: University of Chicago Press.
Feroz, Ahmad
  1969 *The Young Turks: The Committee of Union and Progress in Turkish Politics 1904-1914*. Oxford: Oxford University Press at the Clarendon Press.
Gallagher, Charles F.
  1966 "Contemporary Islam: The Straits of Secularism." American Universities Field Staff Reports Service, Southwest Asia Series, Vol. 15 (3).
Geertz, Clifford
  1963 "The Integrative Revolution." In C. Geertz, ed., *Old Societies and New States: The Quest for Modernity in Asia and Africa*. New York: The Free Press.
Gierke, Otto
  1958 *Political Ideas of the Middle Age*. F.W. Maitland, translator. Boston: Beacon Press.
Gluckman, Max
  1965 *Politics, Law and Ritual in Tribal Society*. Chicago: Aldine.
Gluckman, Max, and E. Devons, Eds.
  1964 *Closed Systems and Open Minds*. Edinburgh: Oliver and Boyd.
Goffman, Erving
  1959 *The Presentation of Self in Everyday Life*. New York: Doubleday Anchor.

Gökalp, Ziya
1959 *Turkish Nationalism and Western Civilization: Selected Essays by Ziya Gökalp.* Translated and edited by Niyazi Berkes. London: Allen and Unwin.
Greenberg, Joseph
1966 *The Languages of Africa.* Bloomington: Indiana University Press.
Halévy, Elie
1955 *The Growth of Philosophical Radicalism.* Boston: Beacon Press.
İpekçi, Abdi, and Ömer Sami Coşar
1965 *İhtilalin İçyüzü (Inside the Coup).* Istanbul: Uygun Yayınevi.
Kaizi, M.
1948 *Kabaka Daudi Cwa: Obulamu, Omulembe n'Ebirowoozo Bye. (Kabaka Daudi Cwa: His Life, Times and Thought).* Kampala: Baganda C.S. Press.
Kant, I.
1786 *The Philosophy of Kant.* Translated and edited by Karl Friedrich. New York: Modern Library, 1949.
Kariuki, J.W.
1963 *"Mau Mau" Detainee.* London: Oxford University Press.
Karpat, Kemal
1959 *Turkey's Politics: The Transition to a Multi-Party System.* Princeton: Princeton University Press.
Kazantzakis, Nikos
1966 *Freedom and Death.* London: Faber and Faber.
Kerr, Clark
1960 "Changing Social Structures." In W.E. Moore and A.S. Feldman, eds., *Labor Commitment and Social Change in Developing Areas.* New York: Social Science Research Council.
Kinross, Lord
1964 *Atatürk: The Rebirth of a Nation.* London: Weidenfeld and Nicholson.
Kohn, Hans
1944 *The Idea of Nationalism.* New York: Macmillan.
Kuhn, Thomas S.
1963 *The Structure of Scientific Revolutions.* Chicago: University of Chicago Press.
Kuran, Ercüment
1967 Lectures on modern Turkish history, given at the Middle East Technical University, Second Semester.
Larimore, Ann Evans
1959 *The Alien Town: Patterns of Settlement in Busoga, Uganda.* Chicago: University of Chicago Department of Geography Research Papers, No. 55.

Lazarsfeld, Paul F., Bernard Berelson, and Hazel Gaudet
   1948 *The Peoples' Choice: How the Voter Makes up His Mind in a Presidential Campaign.* New York: Columbia University Press.
Leslie, J.A.K.
   1963 *A Survey of Dar es Salaam.* London: Oxford University Press on behalf of the East African Institute of Social Reseach.
Levy, Reuben
   1957 *The Social Structure of Islam.* Cambridge: Cambridge University Press.
Lewis, Bernard `
   1961 *The Emergence of Modern Turkey.* London: Oxford University Press under the auspices of the Royal Institute for International Affairs.
Lewis, Charleton T., and Charles Short
   1879 *A Latin Dictionary.* London: Oxford University Press.
Lienhardt, Peter
   1966 "A Controversy over Islamic Custom in Kilwa Kivinje, Tanzania." In I.M. Lewis, ed., *Islam in Tropical Africa.* London: Oxford University Press for the International African Institute.
Lofchie, Michael F.
   1965 *Zanzibar: Background to Revolution.* Princeton: Princeton University Press.
Low, D.A., and R.C. Pratt
   1960 *Buganda and British Overrule.* London: Oxford University Press for the East African Institute of Social Research.
Mayhew, Henry
   1861-62 *London Labor and the London Poor.* New York: Dover Press, facsimile edition, 1968.
Mead, George Herbert
   1934 *Mind, Self and Society.* Chicago: University of Chicago Press.
Mead, Margaret
   1949 *Male and Female.* New York: Morrow.
Medawar, P.B.
   1963 "Onward from Spencer: Evolution and Evolutionism." *Encounter* 21(3):35-43.
Morgan, Lewis Henry
   1871 *Ancient Society.* Edited, with introduction and annotations by Eleanor Burke Leacock. Cleveland: World Publishing Co., 1963.
Morris, H.S.
   1968 *The Indians in Uganda.* Chicago: University of Chicago Press.
Mutesa II, Kabaka of Uganda
   1967 *The Desecration of My Kingdom.* London: Constable.
*New York Times Encyclopedic Almanac*
   1971 New York: New York Times.

Niebuhr, H. Richard
1951 *Christ and Culture.* New York: Harper.
Nisbet, Robert
1969 *Social Change and History.* New York: Oxford University Press.
Okello, John
1967 *Revolution in Zanzibar.* Nairobi: East African Publishing House.
O'Sullivan, John Louis
1845 *United States Magazine and Democratic Review.* July–August.
Özbudun, Ergun
1966 *The Role of the Military in Recent Turkish Politics.* Harvard University Center for International Affairs, Occasional Papers in International Affairs, No. 14.
Parkin, David
1969 *Neighbors and Nationals in an African City Ward.* Berkeley and Los Angeles: University of California Press.
Parsons, Talcott
1937 *The Structure of Social Action.* New York: McGraw-Hill.
1966 *Societies: Evolutionary and Comparative Perspectives.* Englewood Cliffs, N.J.: Prentice-Hall.
1971 *The System of Modern Societies.* Englewood Cliffs, N.J.: Prentice-Hall.
Peacock, James, and Thomas A. Kirsch
1970 *The Human Direction: An Evolutionary Approach.* New York: Appleton-Century-Crofts.
Popper, Karl
1957 *The Poverty of Historicism.* London: Routledge and Kegan Paul.
1946 *The Open Society and Its Enemies.* Princeton: Princeton University Press.
Richards, Audrey
1964 "Traditional Values and Current Political Behavior." In L.A. Fallers, ed., *The King's Men: Authority and Status in Buganda on the Eve of Independence.* London: Oxford University Press on Behalf of the East African Institute of Social Research.
Robinson, Richard D.
1963 *The First Turkish Republic.* Cambridge: Harvard University Press.
Roe, Anne, and George G. Simpson (Eds.)
1958 "Introduction." *Behavior and Evolution.* New Haven: Yale University Press.
Rosberg, C.G., Jr., and John Nottingham
1966 *The Myth of "Mau Mau": Nationalism in Kenya.* New York: Praeger.
Sahlins, Marshall D., and Elman R. Service (Eds.)
1960 *Evolution and Culture.* Ann Arbor: University of Michigan Press.

Schutz, Alfred
   1962 *Collected Papers,* Vol. I. The Hague: Martinus Nijhoff.
   1967 *The Phenomenology of the Social World.* Evanston: Northwestern University Press.
Shils, Edward
   1957 "Primordial, Personal, Sacred and Civil Ties." *British Journal of Sociology* 8 (June):130-145.
   1961 "Centre and Periphery." In *The Logic of Personal Knowledge: Essays Presented to Michael Polanyi on His Seventieth Birthday.* London: Routledge and Kegan Paul.
   1962 *Political Development in the New States.* 's-Gravenhage: Mouton.
Szyliowicz, J.S.
   1966 *Political Change in Rural Turkey: Erdemli.* The Hague: Mouton.
Thomas, W.I.
   1917 "The Persistence of Primary Group Norms in Present-day Society and Their Influence in Our Educational System." In Herbert S. Jennings et al., eds., *Suggestions of Modern Science Concerning Education.* New York: Macmillan.
*Turkish Government Organization Manual*
   1966 English edition. Ankara: Institute of Public Administration for Turkey and the Middle East.
Vryonis, Speros, Jr.
   1971 *The Decline of Medieval Hellenism in Asia Minor and the Process of Islamicization from the Eleventh through the Thirteenth Century.* Berkeley: University of California Press.
Watson, James
   1968 *The Double Helix: A Personal Account of the Discovery of the Structure of DNA.* New York: Atheneum.
Weber, Max
   1958 *The Protestant Ethic and the Spirit of Capitalism.* New York: Scribner.
   1963 *Sociology of Religion.* Boston: Beacon Press.
   1968 *Economy and Society.* New York: Bedminster Press.
Weiker, Walter F.
   1963 *The Turkish Revolution 1960-61.* Washington: The Brookings Institution.
White, Leslie
   1959 *The Evolution of Culture: The Development of Civilization to the Fall of Rome.* New York: McGraw-Hill.
Woodham-Smith, Cecil
   1962 *The Great Hunger: Ireland, 1845-49.* New York: Harper and Row.
Yetkin, Giyas
   1939 *Edremit.* Balıkesir: Türk Pazarı Basımevi.

1957 *Kuruluşundan Bugüne kadar Edremitte olup Bitenler (Events in Edremit from Its Founding to Today)*. Balıkesir: Türkdili Matbaası.
Zanzibar Protectorate
1924 *Report on the Native Census, 1924*. Zanzibar: Government Printer.
1931 *Report on the Census Enumeration of the Whole Population 1931*. Zanzibar: Government Printer.
1953 *Notes on the Census of the Zanzibar Protectorate*. Zanzibar: Government Printer.
1960 *Report on the Census of the Zanzibar Protectorate, 1958*. Zanzibar: Government Printer.

# INDEX

167

THE SOCIAL ANTHROPOLOGY OF THE NATION-STATE
BY LLOYD A. FALLERS

Alexander J. Morin, Publisher
Georganne E. Marsh, Production Editor
Mitzi Carole Trout, Production Manager

Designed by Aldine Staff
Composition by Metrographics, Inc., Chicago, Illinois
Printed by Printing Headquarters, Inc.
  Arlington Heights, Illinois
Bound by Brock & Rankin, Chicago, Illinois